Unwritten
A Love Story

~

Hayley Howell

Lucy,
Thank you for being
such a true, loyal friend!
Love you!
♥ Hayley Howell

Published by Expert Message Group, LLC

Expert Message Group, LLC
5215 East 71st Street
Suite 1400
Tulsa, OK 74136

918.576.7306

www.expertmessagegroup.com

First Printing, August 2011

ISBN 9781936875023

Printed in the United States of America
Set in 11/15.75pt Book Antiqua

For permissions, please contact:

Expert Message Group, LLC
5215 East 71st Street
Suite 1400
Tulsa, OK 74136

For you, Babe

Chapter One

"This is your captain speaking," announced the disembodied voice. "We're fourth in line for take-off, so we're looking at just about ten minutes here on the runway. Time for y'all to get seated and, well, welcome aboard Flight 1030, folks."

Hurry up and wait. I know something about that. You can spend your whole life hustling to get from one place to the next, but more likely than not, all you'll do once you get there is wait. "Be still in the presence of the Lord and wait patiently for him to act," Brian would probably say. I can feel a small smile creep over my lips as my mind fills with the sound of Brian's voice, but the moment is interrupted by my seatmate returning from his second trip to the bathroom. And we haven't even gotten off the ground yet.

"Would you like to sit here instead?" I ask, offering him my aisle seat. "I certainly don't mind a view, and you just might be more comfortable."

"You know, I think that would be a fine idea," says the man. He must be nearing fifty, but he's aging well, and I suspect the creases at the corners of his eyes and sides of his mouth got there from laughing, not crying. I shuffle over to the window seat and am surprised by how grateful I feel to be so near the double-paned glass. It's nice to be one seat closer to heaven.

"Hank," he says, extending his hand.

"Hayley."

"I get a little nervous before I fly, and it makes me feel like I can't drink enough water," he said. "Then I get on the plane and everything's okay, but here I am, running to that tiny bathroom every ten minutes like clockwork."

He has a friendly face, and I know once we're in the air I'll welcome the distraction of conversation with this stranger. I don't want him to be embarrassed about his confession, but there doesn't seem to be much I can say about it. "Where are you from?" I offer instead.

"Owasso," he says, clearly relieved to have the subject changed.

"Me too! Whereabouts?"

"161st Street, right past the park."

I can't believe it, and I tell him so. That's just three blocks over from where I live. Brian has always made a point of telling me that our red and tan brick rancher with the big bay window flanked by black shutters is *his* house, not mine. And I always thank him for graciously letting his wife live there rent-free. I don't tell my new friend that last part, though. Some people just don't understand Brian's humor.

"Well I'll be!" says Hank, and I can tell from the warmth in his eyes that we're as good as long-time neighbors now. "I've got two boys, both grown. I'm on my way to visit the older one out in Colorado. Where are you headed?"

"Arizona."

I don't elaborate too much on that, but before Hank can press me for any details we feel the plane start to gather speed beneath us. I haven't taken too many plane trips in my life, and I don't know if the way I feel about take-off would be any different if I had, but I'm always amazed at the way a big, heavy hunk of metal can hoist itself into the air. It's almost like the work of moving forward on the ground takes so much energy, the thing can't help but celebrate by lifting its nose toward the sky. And by then ... well, by then it might as well get somewhere worth going.

The flight attendants make their announcements about safety and I don't listen too closely. With the way things have been going, I don't see how a crash could make anything much worse. That's "stinkin' thinkin'" as a good friend of mine says, but I can't help it. I look out the window

6

and watch Tulsa fall away mile by mile, until the segmented patches of faded green and brown all blend into each other and I can't tell farm from highway. I wonder if my memories will do something like that as each day passes—merge into one another over time until all I have left is a blob of hazy shapes. Of course, I don't know which would be worse: remembering every grueling hour of the past year, or forgetting a single second.

Eventually the flight attendants come around and Hank treats me to a drink. He doesn't want to drink alone, he says, emptying a tiny bottle of amber liquid into a plastic cup half-filled with soda and ice. That's fine with me; having a drink with a new friend is another "first" I can check off my list, and come to think of it, so is this flight.

People may say there's a first time for everything, but I've learned that "firsts" come in waves. There's the first time you meet a person and go out to dinner, for example, and that's the first time you're sharing a meal. But then there's the first time the two of you dine as a couple; the first time you eat at the kitchen table you share; the first time you break bread as husband and wife. The excitement of doing something for the first time makes those moments special, memorable. But sometimes you find you have to go back to the scene of one of your "firsts"—that same kitchen table, for instance, or that same restaurant. Only now the circumstances have changed and you find yourself there with someone else, or worse, by yourself. So there you are having the same "first" all over again, but instead of feeling excited by this special moment in your life, you feel haunted by the memory of that other first time.

The first time Brian and I ate together was on our first date. I had just come off a shift at Dylan's Western Wear and didn't have time to change out of my uniform—a button-down plaid shirt with contrast stitching, jeans, and boots—before I was supposed to meet Brian at the TGI Friday's down the road from the store. At the time, I told myself, "Hayley, if he thinks you're pretty wearing this, he'll think you're pretty in anything." So I went.

I stop myself from following the trail of memories that I know will leave me breathless. I can't help but smile when I think back on that time, even though lifting the corners of my mouth feels like exercise these days—something my body isn't used to. Things were so simple then, and in the years that followed, when I'd wait for Brian to come home from work smelling like gasoline, then wait some more for him to shower and change so he could sit with me at dinner and tell me about his day. Those were the days when Brian and I would hop into his truck and turn up the radio really loud while we drove to Braum's for Brian's mint chocolate chip shake and my waffle cone twist. Of course, that was before Brian and I got to know the insides of Tower Seven at Hillside Hospital, before we lived and breathed daily blood panel results, before our family dinners meant choking down hospital food from plastic cups and paper plates. Like I said—stinkin' thinkin.'

Smiling was easy back then, before this whole mess started. A grin might spring to my lips unexpectedly at any time, prompted by one of Brian's dry quips or a punch line delivered by a character from one of the shows we liked to watch together. Our life was filled with laughter, love, happiness and passion, and our home was filled with smiles for days because of it.

But everything is different now. Now, with no place to house my heart, I'm not sure I even know where *home* is anymore.

The captain updates us about our altitude—why that should matter to me, I have no idea—but it jolts me out of my daze and I ask Hank about what his son does out in Colorado. That seems to make him happy, and I'm relieved to have a story to listen to. Everything is going fine until Hank mentions a passion he shares with his sons—restoring vintage Corvettes.

"My husband *loves* Corvettes!" The words tumble out before I can stop them, and I regret it right away.

"Well he'll just have to come on over and see what we've got in the garage, then. It's a '67 Convertible with 300 HP. Mariana Blue, they call it, and let me tell you—I don't know how much your husband's told you about Corvettes, but this model is a beauty. You think he'd be interested in takin' a look?"

The panic sets in, an all-too-familiar feeling I get lately when I've made a mistake. I swallow a gulp of my drink that's already turned warm. "Sure," I say, because I don't see how I have any other choice. "He'd love that."

Chapter Two

October 2006 brought a drought through most of Oklahoma, and Owasso was dry as a tinderbox. I was living in an apartment on a short-term lease, trying to figure out what to do with myself. It had been almost four months since I had broken it off with my last boyfriend of eighteen months, and I knew I wanted to find a new relationship with someone ... special. Extraordinary, even. I guess you could say I felt like I was ready for true love.

But how does a girl working one full-time job and one part-time job find the time to meet someone worth meeting? A friend of mine had suggested online dating, but something about that whole process just gave me the creeps. I thought it would be something like shopping for groceries—comparing labels, looking for certain ingredients listed in a profile or a headshot. And there I'd be, just another item on the shelf for someone to pick up, look at, and put back. No, thank you.

I discovered what I thought was a happy medium between putting myself out there for all the world to see, and showing up to the same local hang-outs each week, hoping for something to change: SinglesChat.

SinglesChat let men and women record voice messages that other singles in the area could listen to. And while I was always suspicious of online dating profiles—since really, what's going to stop a man from hiding the truth behind his computer screen?—I liked the idea that it was nearly impossible for a person to fake certain genuine qualities in their voice. I didn't think a man could pretend to have the warmth and compassion I was looking for, or put up a front of easy laughter and kindness. There's some music that just instantly appeals to one person, while it sounds like nails on a chalkboard to someone else, and that's what I was looking for—the man's voice that would be music to my ears.

Or so I thought.

"Hey there, I'm Brian. Thirty-two years old. I know what I'm looking for and … well, I don't want to take care of anybody. So if you're lookin' to be taken care of, well, you're probably not for me."

Is he for real? I thought to myself. I couldn't figure out why this Brian character had left me a message ("Let's talk. Call me at home."), and I was even more shocked when I heard his pre-recorded greeting. *Not too terribly friendly,* I thought. But then again, I'd never been one to dismiss people so easily, and I called him back.

It was already close to ten when I picked up the receiver, but Brian picked up after just the second ring.

"Hayley?"

"Hi, yes—it's Hayley." Hearing him say my name sent a shudder down my spine, and there was something endearing about the way he was obviously waiting by the phone for my call. I could hear the smile creep across his lips as he asked me about my day, my favorite things—color, TV show, food—and my family.

Try as I might to resist, I was curious about how Brian looked. Apparently he was thinking the same thing, because almost at once we suggested swapping pictures. Within minutes, he texted me a snapshot of himself. I remember pausing before clicking the little button that would open the file. "This could be him," I told myself. "This could be the face of the man you spend the rest of your life with. Or not." I laughed at myself just then, because I realized how foolish it was to have put so much stock in a man who was still just a voice on the far side of a phone line.

Right away I noticed the warm glow in his eyes, and something else there, too: a hint of laughter, maybe, like the two of us shared an inside joke the rest of the world was dying to know. Next I noticed the slight tilt of his head, the curve of his lip, and I thought, *Here's a man with confidence, who knows what he wants.* And of course I couldn't have known it then, but I was right.

Before I knew it, I caught a glimpse of a clock boasting a time near 3:00 a.m.

"I've got to be getting to bed," I said, though I hoped he could hear the genuine regret in my voice.

"Okay," he said, suddenly matter-of-fact. "But I'll be givin' you a call tomorrow."

"A little earlier?" I asked.

"A little."

"Well goodnight, then, Brian."

"Sweet dreams."

He did call the next day. And the day after that. And before I knew it, almost a week had gone by, and Brian said he wanted to meet.

Now there's nothing but sky as far as the eye can see, and I'm feeling especially thankful to be sitting near the window. The clouds below look like a blanket of soft white, and I can't help but wonder what it would feel like to drift through the air, passing through those great tufts on the way down . . .

Remembering is hard. At first it feels good to remember, like I could float around all day in those simpler times. Just like the clouds outside my window, the memories seem solid enough to support me, real enough to keep me afloat for as long as I can keep on thinking. But eventually clouds turn to rain, and drop by drop they fall out of the sky like tears until there is nothing left at all. And that's just like me, too: tear by tear, I feel like I'm dissolving into someone I don't recognize anymore. If I could find a way to stop crying, there might just be hope that I could piece myself together again.

I'm suddenly self-conscious before I realize that Hank has fallen asleep and can't see the little round tearstains on my shirt. I wish I could sleep, too. But sleep means dreaming, and dreams can turn on a dime, so before you know it you're trapped in a nightmare where you keep reliving the moments in your life you'd most like to forget. I force down those thoughts and gaze out the window again, and let my mind fill with memories as big and beautiful as the clouds just beyond the wing.

I saw Brian sitting at that bar, and believe it or not, my first thought was, *Hmm … I'm just not sure he's really my type.* He seemed almost *soft* around the edges, and that's when I realized I'd made him out in my mind to be some kind of buff, body-building gym rat. Talking to him for the past week had put a picture in my head of someone strong enough to haul gasoline all day, work on his house at night, and ride one of the fastest bikes in the world—a ZX14—on the weekends.

I couldn't say for sure what we talked about that night, but we shared an appetizer and a few rounds of drinks and before I knew it, Brian was holding my coat for me and guiding me to the door. "Would you like to come over?" he asked me. I was shocked by how casual he seemed, like I had been over to his place a dozen times or more. And I was even more amazed that he thought I was "that" kind of girl—the kind that goes over to a man's house when she has only just met him.

"I—" I started, trying to find a polite way to take my leave.

"I know," he interrupted. "I know it's … odd. And even though it sounds like a line, I can promise you I've never done this before. I just … I was hoping you'd … well—"

While we were both standing there speechless, I was a little ashamed to admit to myself that going home with Brian was exactly what I wanted to do. In fact, I was suddenly overcome by the feeling that I'd regret it awfully for the rest of my life if I did anything else.

"Okay," I said, and I could practically see the relief spread over his features. "But I've got a dog at home I've got to take care of, and I need to grab some clothes."

"I'll follow you."

"That's fine," I said, reaching for my keys. "But I'll warn you now—I drive fast."

And I did. So fast, in fact, that a police car driving in the opposite direction flashed his lights at me as a warning to slow down. I never heard the end of that from Brian, who I learned was something of a stickler for the rules, and it started the moment we stepped out of our respective vehicles in front of my apartment building.

"We could have gotten in a heck of a lot of trouble if he'd decided to stop you," he scolded.

"Oh, would *we* have been in trouble?" I said, and right away I could see my flirtatiousness made him blush.

"Just get your things and let's get going."

"Fine," I said, "but I should warn you about Zoe. She's a Min Pin, and she doesn't much like strangers."

"All dogs love me," he insisted.

"Well just don't say you weren't warned."

Even though I'm almost compulsively tidy, I was anxious about having Brian in the apartment before I'd had time to clean up. I waved him to the living room, where Zoe loudly protested the presence of our guest, then excused myself to the bedroom to pack a few things. I was close to having everything I thought I'd need stuffed into a WalMart sack when I heard a yell—and a string of expletives—coming from the living room.

"What in the name—" I started to say, but as soon as I rounded the corner to the living room I saw what had happened, clear as day. There was Zoe, sitting as politely as an altar boy in church on Easter, watching Brian cradle his right hand in his left as he stared down my little dog as though she were Satan himself.

"She drew blood!" he said by way of explanation, but I just laughed and rolled my eyes.

"I told you she doesn't like people."

"Are you ready to go yet?"

"Yeah," I said. "I'm ready."

I was forced to temper my speed on the way to Brian's house, what with him setting the pace in his big black Sierra, and being alone in the car gave me time to think about what was happening. The past few hours seemed to have gone by at top speed, and I felt almost helpless by how unexpectedly smitten I felt. My heart was racing in my chest, I couldn't wipe the stupid grin from my face, and I could feel myself blushing every time Brian looked at me with those big baby blue eyes. Mixed in with it all was a sense of what I can only describe as regret—that we were only just meeting now, that I had ever wasted time seeing anyone else, that some other woman had already married and divorced Brian. I was upset by the possibility that the experience might have left Brian jaded, but then I had to scold myself for letting my mind run away with the situation like that. After all, I had only just met Brian. Why was I so anxious about the time we hadn't spent together, when I could count on one hand the number of hours we had?

Any confusion I was feeling flew right out of my head the moment I realized we had arrived at Brian's place. I was stunned by the sweet house positioned on a neatly manicured lawn. A sconce near the front door beckoned to me like the scent of warm apple pie. *"Home,"* I thought I heard it whisper. *"Home."*

I couldn't believe that a man who staunchly claimed to have no interest at all in taking care of a woman would bother owning a house like that, but I didn't say anything as he led me on a tour from room to room. Every detail of the place felt intentional, and Brian told me he had decided on specifics from wall placement to wall color and everything in between. I could feel how proud he was of the house he had built, and rightfully so.

"This here," Brian said, approaching the last door at the end of a short hallway, "this is my room." I remember being struck by what a silly thing that was to say—the whole house was his house, so of course every room was his room. But when Brian slipped his hand into mine, I could feel that we shared the same nervous excitement, the same anxious anticipation. His grip was hot but soft, and I felt a ripple of chills move up my arm and a shiver ran down the whole left side of my body.

We were both tentative at first, as we peeled back layer after layer of our histories, the stories and experiences that made us who we were. I felt a powerful, compelling need to reveal everything to Brian, to expose my secrets one by one. This person, I thought to myself—this person has to know *everything* about me. Our conversations that night touched on everything from past relationships to faith to family, and I felt like I was getting to see a side of Brian that few people ever had, or would. Wrapped in his embrace, I felt safe enough to confide my secrets, my hopes and dreams. Just as we were drifting off to sleep, he asked me a final question.

"What do you want to be when you grow up?" he whispered playfully. His lips lingered over the place on my neck just below my ear.

"A good wife and mother," I answered drowsily.

He seemed to think about that for a moment, then: "Good night, babe."

"Good night, babe," I said, slipping into the nickname like an old pair of jeans. And just as I felt myself floating into dreamland, I thought how funny it was that we were already using such a term of endearment— like we had been lying in each other's arms for years.

Chapter Three

After that first night, Brian and I never spent an evening apart. It was like we had fallen into lives we'd been living for a long time—as though we had both stepped into a fast-moving river that swept us up and carried us along like dry leaves on the surface of the water. By the week's end, Brian pulled me into his arms and, with a self-consciousness I would come to know as one of his more beautiful qualities, whispered, "You're my girlfriend now, right?" And I was.

November had crept in almost overnight, and there was a bite to the air that felt fresh and cold in my lungs. Brian teased me endlessly about how it seemed I was moving in with him "Walmart sack by Walmart sack," since each night I'd come through the door weighed down by the telltale white and blue bags. When I mentioned that my lease was due to expire at the month's end, Brian casually suggested that I not renew. "Okay," I said, with what I hoped was pragmatic indifference. Inside, my heart soared.

Around the middle of that month, Brian and I headed to my cousin Sherry's apartment. She and Brian hadn't met yet, and even though she was newly divorced and not in the best of spirits, I was eager for my whole family to meet the new man in my life. Almost as soon as we settled ourselves around Sherry's living room for drinks, she started going on and on about how differently she'd do marriage the next time around.

"Between you and me," she said conspiratorially, "my next husband better have a bank roll with room for one more—if you know what I mean."

I wasn't sure I did, but Sherry continued without prompting from either of us. In fact, she seemed to respond to Brian's stony silence by jabbering incessantly about her "ideal man."

"I won't be settling for no tiny speck of a diamond, either," she spat. "I want a *rock*. A legitimately huge *rock*. I want a big house, a nice car, vacations twice a year. I want to be wined and dined, you know? Because that's what I *deserve*, you know? Someone who can really take care of me. Someone who's not afraid to be a man and lavish me with the finer things in life. *You know?*"

It took a few seconds for me to realize that Sherry was looking at me expectantly, clearly waiting for me to validate her new vision of marital bliss. "Sure, sure, I know," I said. "You want what you want. You want nice things. That's understandable."

"No, not just 'nice things,' Hayley—I want a nice man to *give* me nice things. I could get nice things on my own eventually, but what I want—what I *need*—is someone to provide those things on my behalf. You understand?"

"Completely."

"What about you, Brian? You understand what kind of man my cousin needs? Because we don't need no more losers signing up as husbands in this family."

I felt a sinking feeling in my stomach as Brian forced a smile and nodded. "I hear you loud and clear," he managed. I knew he must be uncomfortable with how personal Sherry was getting, with them having only just met. I was learning that Brian was shy around other people—or rather, I was learning that Brian was a private man who assumed others wanted privacy, too. Even sitting on that couch, he kept a little distance between us; "I'm not into PDA," he had told me early on. So while privately I could count on this man to hold me tight and kiss me hard and tell me everything that popped into his head, in public he kept his hands and thoughts to himself.

18

The conversation eventually steered itself to safer waters—work and the weather, local news and stories from all our younger years—and Brian seemed to warm up a little despite Sherry's brazen introduction. At the end of the night, I dozed in the car as Brian drove us back to his house, and when we got there we were both so tired we didn't have much time to talk. The next morning Brian kissed me goodbye like he always did, and I got on with my day as usual.

Everything was fine until noon.

In what had quickly become a daily routine, I called Brian on my lunch break. He sounded … distant.

"What's wrong, babe?" I asked. I thought maybe he'd gotten word about a bad shift change or something.

"I don't think this is going to work out."

"Babe, you know we can work around any schedule you get. It's not like—"

"No, Hayley. Listen. *I don't think this is going to work out.*"

He can't be talking about us, I thought, but in that same moment, the realization hit me like a million tons of bricks stacked on the back of an eighteen-wheeler.

"Are you saying … are you breaking up with me?" I said, hanging onto my incredulity like a life preserver.

"I'm sorry, Hayley, I truly am. It's just … I just don't think it's gonna work out."

To this day I don't know how I silenced the sirens blaring in my head long enough to say what I said next, but somehow I managed to get him to agree to let me come over to the house that night. At first he protested, saying it would just make things harder, but I insisted and insisted until he finally relented. When we hung up, I wasn't sure yet what I would say or do when I saw Brian later that night, and I was annoyed that snippets from last night's conversation kept playing in my mind when I tried to focus on the speech I would have to deliver.

Then it hit me.

All Sherry's talk about her "ideal man"—and her assumption that I shared her vision—must have spooked Brian to his very core. My mind reeled back to Brian's message on SinglesChat—the message he chose to broadcast to any potential girlfriends: *". . . I don't want to take care of anybody. So if you're lookin' to be taken care of, well, you're probably not for me."* Of course, Brian's actions had belied the caveat—he was the most caring, considerate man I had ever met. The truth was, Brian wanted to take care of someone—he just didn't want to take care of someone who *expected* to be taken care of. He always said how much he liked my independence, and the fact that, like him, I never took a handout. These were principles we shared and cherished, and Sherry … well, I cursed Sherry in that moment for opening her big mouth, but cursed myself too, for not objecting to the ideas I had never in my life agreed with.

The damage was done, as far as I could tell. Even in our short time together, I had come to know Brian as a man who stuck to his guns once he had made a decision. Hell or high water couldn't turn him back from a path he chose, and all I could do was count the minutes until 5 o' clock, when I told myself I'd drive faster than a lightning strike to get to the man I loved before it was too late. That is, if I wasn't long past too late already.

I look at my face in the airplane bathroom mirror and I wonder about the stranger I see. Why are her eyes so sunken, the shadows beneath them so dark? Why does it seem like her shoulders bear the weight of a heavy burden? Why are her eyes brimming with unshed tears?

As I root through my purse for a lip balm—the air on the plane is so dry—my fingers scrape the bottom of the bag and I feel them catch on the edge of a wallet-sized photograph. I palm it gently without pulling it out of the bag. I don't have to look at it to know exactly what I can see there. Brian and me, our faces round and smooth, our eyes glowing, my cheek pressed against his chest. He's standing there in his baby blue button-down, and I am dressed in white. I'll never forget that day no matter how long I live, but for now I force the memory back inside the box in my mind where I keep precious things, and let the picture fall from my hand, back down into the shadows.

I give up on my appearance for the moment, suddenly weary, and make my way back to my seat.

"Don't say anything," I demanded, and my voice sounded different to me—foreign. It was a voice filled with many things: desperation and fear, longing and love. I hoped it was a voice I could trust to say what I wanted to say, what needed to be said.

"I don't know what happened to you last night, but I suspect some things were said that reminded you of another time, another woman, another relationship. And you know what? I can't help your past, and I can't help what you're afraid of. What I can help you see is that I don't want the ring, or the big house, or the money. All I want is to be a good wife and a good mom. I want to love somebody with all my heart and give my whole soul to someone who will take care of it like I'll take care of his, and I want to live a long time together and make babies and—"

I interrupted myself to catch the breath I hadn't realized I had lost. I saw a funny look on Brian's face and couldn't decide what was hidden behind his eyes, but decided in a flash that I'd keep talking until I was sure I had gotten through to him. I knew I was begging this man to be with me, and I also knew I was waiting for some kind of sign. I just hadn't a clue what it would look like.

"I think you are … amazing," I continued, and I hoped I sounded more in control than I felt. "I really like you. *Really*. And I want this—us—to work. And quite frankly, I always get what I want."

That last line took us both by surprise, and Brian's eyebrows shot up halfway to heaven. I felt myself blush, and I was afraid I had just undone all my speech-making with a single silly sentence. "Well?" I said, finally resigned to whatever fate I had sealed for myself. "Are you gonna say something?"

Brian took a deep breath and let it out, and when he spoke his voice was slow and quiet in a way that made me lean closer so I wouldn't miss a word.

21

"I can say for certain that no one has ever—*ever*—fought for me the way you're fighting for me right now." He seemed to be rolling the idea around in his head like it was a flavor he'd never tasted before. "So I guess what I have to say is … will you be my girlfriend again?"

"Yes!" I squealed, and about leapt into his arms. We kissed and laughed and held each other, and suddenly there was Brian's warm hand, brushing tears from my cheeks.

"You always get what you want, huh?" he whispered.

With my ear pressed to his chest, I could hear his heart beating, and since I felt like I had talked enough for the moment, I just nodded my head.

"And what you want is …"

"You," I whispered, and I squeezed him tighter for emphasis.

"Me." There was a note of finality in Brian's voice, like me wanting him was an idea that had suddenly taken on a whole new shape in his mind.

"I love you, Hayley."

"I love you too, babe."

Just a short time later, the end of the month arrived, and I gave up my apartment and moved in with Brian. His house was already filled with beautiful things, and my move was really just a matter of making room in the closet and drawers and putting up a few pictures of me and my mom. And there was one other thing—a plaque I had seen a while ago in a home goods store that read: *"Dream as if you will live forever, live as if you only have today."* Brian sweetly obliged when I asked him to hang it where we'd see it daily, right above our bed.

Chapter Four

It was only a joke, but when my mom came down to stay with us around Christmas that year and asked Brian how long he planned to keep us "livin' in sin," he colored so deeply I thought he'd never turn back to pale. I swear it was a good-natured rib—my mom liked Brian and was happy we had found each other—but he ushered us out of the house one morning to go down to Moody's and get my ring size.

The forecast called for snow later in the day, and the clouds overhead looked heavy with their burden, like a thick down comforter being used to carry stones. Moody's wasn't as crowded as I thought it would be with Christmas just a few days away—mom and I practically had the whole store to ourselves. We roamed from case to case looking at beautiful jewelry we'd never think to buy because of the expense or the extravagance—or both.

"Can I help you find something specific today? A gift, maybe?" The salesman wore a dark navy suit over a pressed white Oxford, and even his slim, silver tie clip seemed poised.

"I'm just here to get my ring size," I said.

"Of course, just a moment." He disappeared behind a desk in the corner and came back a few moments later with what looked like a giant key ring. From it hung long, thin metal rods, and on the end of each of those was a small ring. Expertly, he slipped a few different rings over the fourth finger on my left hand—too small, too big, just right—and I was suddenly struck by the idea that I had kept that finger empty for so long out of a superstition I didn't know I carried.

"Do you see anything you like?" he asked.

"Oh, I'm not here to look, really," I said, but my eyes followed the sweep of his hand to a case on my left.

And there it was.

The most lovely ring I had ever seen—a princess-cut stone flanked by thin square-cut diamonds in an art deco style that reminded me of Ava Gardner, black-and-white movies, soft-shoe dancing, and heady romance—was resting inconspicuously on a white leather stand.

"Which one?" the salesman asked, with a sureness I knew came from years of seeing women just like me find what they didn't know they were looking for in those pristine cases.

"Yeah, which one?" echoed my mom, suddenly beside me.

"*That* one."

The salesman unlocked the case and from somewhere unseen produced a black velvet display platform to rest the ring on. Examining the piece more closely, I could see the white gold setting just below the center diamond was engraved with delicate hearts. He gestured for me to pick it up and try it on, and only after I had held my hand at arm's length and admired the sparkling stones against my skin did I have the courage to ask the question I knew had to come next.

"And how much is this ring?" I said tentatively.

"$10,995," he said, "plus tax."

As a girl, I had never really projected myself into the stories of princesses, knights, and dragons slain by a gallant young hero; maybe I had somehow known that those kinds of stories don't happen in real life, at least not *my* real life. Trying on that ring and hearing how much it cost—as much as the better part of a brand new car or a down payment on a house—confirmed my suspicion that I'd never be the damsel in a fairy tale, destined for bedazzling jewels and fancy dresses. I felt deflated but resigned; it was such a beautiful ring, and I guess I thought it would be nice to feel like wanting something that nice was okay.

"Let me give you a hint card," offered the salesman.

"That would be great," my mom chimed.

"Oh, no," I said. "He would rip me a new one!" Neither of them knew that Brian had nearly ended our relationship over just this type of thing, and even though he had sent me off to get my ring size, I didn't want to push my luck. I knew I'd be happy with whatever ring he chose, since it would mean he and I were headed to forever. The idea brought a smile to my lips that the salesman took for consent, and before I knew it he was pressing a small card into my hand with the ring description, price, and my size filled out in small, neat script.

All the way home in the car I debated whether I should just tell Brian my ring size without handing him the hint card, but my mom made it clear she'd tell him I'd seen something I liked if I didn't give him the card myself.

"Are you kidding me?" Brian exclaimed when I handed him the rectangular slip of paper. I winced with embarrassment and instantly regretted giving in to my mom and the salesman. After the whole incident with Sherry, I had promised myself I would do more standing up for myself and less going along with other people's bad advice. "You're insane!" he pronounced. Someone mercifully changed the subject, and that seemed to be the end of *that* conversation.

The whole rest of that day and the next I kept my eye on Brian for signs that we were headed for an argument about that stupid ring, or worse, another breakup. But when Brian didn't say anything else, I supposed he had just vowed to forget the whole matter, and within a week, I knew I was in the clear.

A couple months later, in February, I found myself near Moody's again, though I didn't dare go inside. I was at a strip mall a mile down the road, shopping for Brian's Valentine's Day gift. We had agreed not to go crazy with gifts—Christmas had only just passed, and spending money on trinkets was never our way. I had already picked out the perfect card, one that said how I felt but left room for me to write a good-sized note myself, and was wandering the card store for inspiration.

I didn't have any idea what to get Brian. We already lived in a house full of things, he had all the clothes he needed, and his bike and truck were in perfect condition. I thought of getting him a gift certificate for detail work on one of the vehicles, but realized Brian might not want to leave the job up to a stranger. I had a mind to make him a key chain with our picture and an inscription—he was always on the road, after all, and it would be something he could keep with him when he was away from home. It was a good idea, I thought—a mall in Tulsa would be my next stop.

I had wandered over to a shelf of knick-knacks and was absentmindedly picking up and putting down the toys and gifts arranged there. I was startled from my thoughts by a deep voice coming from a plush in my hands; it was two green frogs sitting face-to-face with their arms wrapped around one another, and when I pulled their froggy lips apart, a rumbling bass said "Kissss meeee!" before the sound of lips smacking punctuated the sentiment.

It was perfect.

I headed home to tidy up and get ready. Brian had made reservations at Charleston's for dinner the night of the 10th since he'd be working on the 14th. I thought it a bit odd that he was taking our early Valentine's Day celebration so seriously—we rarely made reservations for our favorite local restaurant—but I was looking forward to reading whatever card he'd gotten for me, and I didn't protest the formality.

When Brian got home that night, he showered and changed as usual, but seemed … *off.* I chalked it up to workday stress and tried to herd him out the door in time for us to have a drink at the bar before sitting down to eat.

"What are you in such a rush for?" Brian asked. "There's two bottles of wine in the fridge. Let's have a drink before we go."

"Well that's just what I was thinking," I started to say, "only I thought we could go to Charleston's and—"

"Just open one of the bottles, okay?" he said. "And gifts. Let's open gifts now."

I once again attributed his abruptness to work stress, and though I didn't say it, I thought, *Yes, one of us really does need a drink, don't we?* I retrieved a bottle from the fridge, opened it, and returned to the living room with two glasses and a renewed resolve not to let Brian's mood ruin our evening. But the couch was empty—Brian was nowhere to be seen.

I heard a loud creak and a soft thud, and recognized the sound of the attic door above the garage swinging closed. Brian came back into the house looking flustered, and his face was so flushed I thought he might be feeling sick. The burgundy bag he was holding seemed to vibrate slightly, and I realized Brian's hands were shaking uncontrollably.

"Babe? Are you okay?" I asked, genuinely alarmed.

He didn't answer but came straight to the couch and sat down. I poured our wine—I didn't trust Brian's hands to aim well enough to fill our glasses—and Brian started to talk as I settled in next to him.

"Before I give you your present, I just want to ask you … do you for sure like me?"

"Well, *yeah*," I said, and I hoped my tone conveyed how I thought this was an obvious answer to an unnecessary question. And then, for good measure and because he just seemed so darn anxious, "I love you, you know that. Why are you asking?"

"Because," he said, pulling a small box from the bag and lowering himself onto one knee, "I just want to know for sure that you'll always be there for me. I want to know that you'll be by my side so we can face our lives together, that you care about me as much as I care about you." Brian was tearing up now, and I remember having something like an out-of-body experience as the enormity of the situation started to make itself clear.

"There's a card in there that says it better than I can, Hayley, but what I mean is that I want to spend the rest of my life being the best thing that's ever happened to you. Will you marry me?"

Then came the sound of tiny hinges and a lid popping open, and when I blinked back the tears that had filled my eyes and lowered my gaze to the box in Brian's hand, I saw it.

The ring.

My ring.

Of course I said "yes"—in fact, I said it again and again—and Brian slipped that beautiful ring onto my finger and we held each other so tight the whole world could have fallen away and we'd still have had something to cling to. You can imagine I felt like a fool handing Brian my gift for him, but he laughed and said he loved it, and propped the kissing frogs on the mantle where everyone would be able to see them.

The whole night was riddled with emotions: surprise and elation, joy and relief, overwhelming love and awe for my husband-to-be. I called my mom to tell her, but she already knew; Brian had asked for her permission to propose weeks before. At the restaurant, I tried to express my disbelief and gratitude that Brian had gotten the ring that I had found so strikingly beautiful.

"I went the very next day," he said, and a mischievous grin spread across his face. "The salesman remembered you. I've had it in the attic ever since."

As amazed as I had been at Brian's proposal, I was even more shocked by this bit of news. I couldn't trust my voice—I had already cried twice in the car on the way over—so I slid my hand across the table and wrapped my fingers around the back of Brian's palm. He covered my hand with his own and gave a little squeeze, and I knew he knew exactly what was in my heart.

Sitting there at Charleston's, I suddenly felt like the envy of every fairy tale princess that had ever been written into existence. They could have their kingdoms and princes and castles in the clouds; in that moment, I had everything I had ever wanted with a better man than I could have ever imagined. "Once upon a time" and "far, far away" could never come close to right here, right now.

My heart fills with a heavy kind of gladness when I look down at my left ring finger and see it there, the ring Brian slipped on my finger just three years ago. The way I've been feeling lately, that night could have been yesterday or a lifetime ago—memories crash into one another and wash over me like waves on the shore, then drag what's left of my resolve out to some deep, dark abyss somewhere. One minute I'm steady on the ground beneath my feet, and in the next I realize the shifting sands have thrown me off balance and into the past.

My right hand fumbles to clutch a heavy pendant hanging at the bottom of a short chain around my neck. It's a pewter disk that says, "*Believe in love,*" not that I really need to be reminded. In fact, belief is one of the only things I can rely on these days.

I slip my index finger through the center of the disk, then let my thumb trace its beveled perimeter. Next I wrap my palm around the pendant and the large metal band that surrounds it. Brian's ring. The disk fits perfectly inside it, the exact circumference of Brian's finger. The metal feels cool against my warm palms, and even though the sensation is refreshing, it's a stark reminder that rings around fingers always feel a little warm.

Believe in love. Brian and I eloped on April 15, 2008. It wasn't one of those elopements that comes as a surprise to family and friends; everyone knew about our plans to head up to Eureka Springs for a private ceremony at a peaceful little retreat center. We had our own bungalow with a hot tub, and the cute old lady who ran the place with her husband was actually an ordained minister. She led the service that officially joined Brian and I as "man and wife," while her husband snapped photos and managed a video recorder on a tripod. The picture in my purse was taken that day, and so was the 8x10 duplicate I've kept framed next to my bed ever since.

That night, we went to a ho-down in town, and the next day we visited the Onyx Caves. The whole weekend, we'd catch each other staring at our wedding bands like they were new appendages, extra fingers we'd suddenly have to learn to use. Now I rub the empty space behind my engagement ring and it seems like the absence is an amputation.

My right hand slides to the third and final circle hanging at the notch in my throat—my own wedding ring. I catch myself thinking how perfect it would be if my ring could fit inside the "*Believe in love*" pendant, so Brian's ring, the charm, and my ring would all fit together in concentric circles. But I scold myself for even entertaining such a thought; the only perfect scenario for our rings is to have them back where they belong, on our fingers.

Believe in love. I'm finding it more and more difficult each day to believe in anything else.

Chapter Five

"Folks, we're just about over Albuquerque, New Mexico ... and we're about 330 miles from our stop in Phoenix. Your flight attendants will be announcing connecting flight gates at Sky Harbor shortly before landing ..."

I tune the captain out once it is clear that the information is irrelevant to me. There was a time, of course, when Brian would have hushed me so we could hear every word of an announcement—as I said, Brian was something of a stickler for the rules—but months ago I developed an inability to process information that didn't pertain directly to our situation. *Our situation.* Makes it seem all neat and tidy, like "our situation" is having too many friends and not enough ice at the party we're throwing to celebrate having too much money. I smirk at the reemergence of my old friend, Mr. Stinkin' Thinkin.'

I feel my memories circling back to the day in 2009 when I suppose you could say "our situation" started to coalesce around a series of sequential events. *Series of sequential events.* Makes it seem all neat and tidy, and not like chaos at all.

December 25, 2009 found us at Brian's mom's house in Bartlesville. Cheryl and Harold, Brian's step-dad, upheld the tradition of Christmas dinner with a bit of a twist: taco night. Brian's favorite. Brian was in charge of frying up the shells, Harold would sauté the meat with chopped onions, garlic, and spices, and Cheryl would methodically lay out the toppings: diced tomatoes, shredded cheese, iceberg lettuce, guacamole, salsa and sour cream. Usually, I'd be catching up with Steve and Stephanie while the kitchen bustled with activity, but that year a blizzard kept Brian's brother and his wife—and their three kids, Jacob, Preston and Hope—from coming down.

Brian had been keeping an eye on the weather all through the evening, and by the time we finished dinner, he was ready to hustle me into the truck for what he suspected would be a treacherous drive home. I never worried about getting where we were going when Brian was at the wheel, though; he and that truck were like one big driving machine, perfectly in sync no matter the conditions. Even so, the snow outside was falling thick and fast, and we only passed a handful of cars as we crawled toward home.

As it had in practically every quiet moment for the last six months, my mind turned to the subject of babies during the drive. And not just babies in general, either—it was the *conceiving* of babies I was particularly concerned with. Brian and I had been trying for what seemed like forever, and every month was a new heartache when I thought I was, but wasn't. I grew up thinking the way I suppose a lot of women do— that when I was ready to have a baby, all I'd have to do is stop trying not to get pregnant and *poof!*—baby makes three.

Brian wasn't worried. He felt in his heart that when we were ready to have a baby, I'd be pregnant. "But if we hope for what we do not have," he'd quote, "we wait for it patiently." I admired Brian for his Bible study and secretly liked to brag about the fact that he had read the whole thing, cover to cover, not once but twice. I usually liked his references to Romans the best, but in this case I wanted a little less preachin' and a lot more … a lot more … heck, I just wanted a baby. I told Brian that come the new year, I wanted us both to go get checked out by a doctor who could shed some light on why this thing—the one thing, in my mind, that would make our lives together even more blissful—seemed to be out of reach.

That night on the car ride home, I was busy thinking about what day would be most convenient for Brian and me to go to the doctor together, when I felt the truck slow to a hesitant stop.

"Whatcha doing, babe?" I asked, taking in my surroundings. Snow had transformed the world into a sparkling wonderland. Twinkle lights and the soft glow from square window panes threw swathes of light over the ground. I realized we were just three houses away from our own, but for some reason Brian was shutting down the engine.

"Sorry, babe, but we're stuck."

"Stuck? That's ridiculous. I can see our house from here." But the truth was, I couldn't. The snow had steadily increased until it seemed there was a solid sheet of white in front of us.

"Well, I can't," said Brian. "And even if I could, the tires are caked. I'm lucky I got over to what I'm guessing is the curb. Bundle up, babe—we're making a dash for it!"

Brian's smile dissolved any annoyance I might have been feeling like hot water in a bowl of sugar, and suddenly we were trudging through the abandoned street together, holding hands and laughing like kids on an adventure in a blustery theme park.

The next morning, we trekked back out to the truck for the less-fun adventure of digging it out. Almost as soon as we got back inside, Brian started walking in the peculiarly sideways style that let me know he'd thrown his back out ... again. In fact, Brian's annual back injuries showed up so consistently, it felt like we were falling into a routine: Brian trudged his way to the bedroom to find whatever position would allow him the most peace, and I filled a hot water bottle and brought it to him, along with some ibuprofen and a can of Diet Mountain Dew, his soda of choice.

Two days later, Brian wasn't feeling a lick better. In fact, it seemed like his pain was getting worse. I took him to the Urgent Care Center at our local hospital, Saint Mary's. In these situations—because they were old hat to Brian, after all—Brian always made sure to tell his doctors that he wasn't a drug seeker. "I just need some Somas and some Lortabs for a week and I'll be fine." It only occurred to me after the fact that doctors might think that's just the kind of thing a drug seeker might say, but Brian always took others' honesty at face value and expected the same in return. Our doctor wanted to order an MRI, but Brian refused; he didn't see a reason to make a fuss over routine back pain. We filled his prescriptions, I drove us home, and back to bed Brian went.

During the following week, the drugs barely got Brian through the day. He'd wake up exhausted despite the heavy sleep he seemed to be getting from the pain medicine, and spent his days gritting his teeth through excruciating discomfort in his back and now, his legs. Every night, he'd hobble to the shower then get into bed, and I'd bring our dinner to the bedroom so we could eat together. By Friday, Brian was so uncomfortable it was making me scared—I thought he might have a slipped disk or pinched a nerve or worse—and as I drifted off to sleep that night, I resolved to get Brian back to the doctor first thing Monday morning.

I dreamed of the woods that night. I was walking through a dense forest, but I wasn't afraid. My feet felt sure beneath me, and I could hear the ambient song of birds and rustling leaves. Dappled light covered the ground as it filtered through a bright green canopy, and I heard laughter—my laughter—like a sweet bell ringing its first note. I was looking for something—no, someone—and I knew it was Brian before I heard myself call out his name. He wasn't lost, though. He was hiding. We were playing a game, and all I had to do was—

Bang! Bang! Bang!

A dull thump reverberated through the forest, almost like someone was driving an axe into the thick bark of an old oak.

Bang! Bang! Bang!

Louder this time.

Bang! Bang! Hayl—

"—ey! Hayley, can you hear me?"

I woke with a start and felt my heart rate quicken. Like anyone interrupted from a deep sleep, I tried to take in the situation around me instantly, tried to absorb my surroundings despite the dark.

"Hayley, are you up? Help, I—"

Brian. Brian was calling me. He wasn't next to me anymore, but I could feel damp heat coming from his side of the bed.

"Babe?" I called, fumbling for the bedside lamp. I squinted against the light and took in the scene: there was Brian, slumped on the floor by the wall. He was glistening with sweat.

"Babe, I can't—I can't find the bathroom. Please help me. I can't—" The effort of speaking seemed to overcome him completely and his voice trailed off.

I was up and over to him as fast as my feet would carry me. "Babe, it's right here—right here," I said, helping him up and over to the door that wasn't two feet from where he sat.

Something was wrong. I mean *really* wrong. Brian was moving and talking like he was drunk or something, but we hadn't had so much as a sip with dinner. Could he have taken too many of his pain pills? I knew for certain that I had given him the right dose before bed, and the bottles were on our bureau, not his nightstand, so there's no way he could have fumbled for another dose in the dark and gotten it wrong— he would have had to wake me up. And then there was the sweat. Since November, there had been several nights when Brian had to get up and towel off, he was so sweaty. He had chalked it up to getting too tangled in our thick flannel sheets, but seeing him soaked through, totally disoriented, clearly in pain—I was scared.

"Babe, something's not right ..." I started to say.

"I'm sorry," he mumbled. "I'm sorry, I'm sorry ..."

I helped Brian back to bed and spent the rest of the night fighting sleep. I wanted to watch over Brian, but caught myself jerking awake again and again.

The next morning, the whole episode took on the weird quality of a dream. Neither of us knew what to say about what had happened, so we said nothing.

After the weekend passed without another incident—but with no improvement in Brian's pain—I took the day off on Monday and got Brian back to Saint Mary's ER. We went through all the same motions with a different doctor and were sent away with the same ineffectual "treatment." When I woke up Tuesday to the sound of my alarm—instead of the sound of Brian brushing his teeth, like usual—I knew he must still be feeling really bad.

"Something's not right," he whispered to me as I leaned in to give him a goodbye kiss.

"I know, babe," I said, "but we'll get you fixed up soon. I promise."

By mid-afternoon I was so worried about Brian that I left work early. When I got home, Brian was practically winded by how much pain he was in. "It's like someone's stabbing me in the back of my legs," he managed to say. I called the ER to let them know we were coming back.

Getting Brian in the car was ... awful. There's no other way to describe it. It was obvious that every step brought him unspeakable discomfort, and my big, strong husband was forced to lean almost all his weight on his little wife.

"We were just here yesterday," I said to the doctor. The face above the white coat was unfamiliar; neither of the other two physicians we had seen at Saint Mary's was available. "Something isn't *right*. In fact, something's very obviously *wrong*, and I want to know what you can do to help my husband."

What they did was pump Brian so full of drugs he couldn't walk. No one offered to help me, so I pulled an abandoned wheelchair from an empty hallway and somehow wrangled Brian—all 270 pounds of him—into the car.

The next week was another lesson in disappointment, with visits to a specialist, a steroid injection in Brian's spine, a failed back brace and a physical therapy session that only seemed to make things worse. Watching that was the last straw for me.

I called Cheryl.

"Tomorrow something has to be done," I said, and I could tell she was surprised to hear the aggressive, matter-of-fact tone in my voice. To be honest, I was, too. But since Christmas, I had slowly been building to this, like a lioness in a jungle surrounded by predators who were hurting us by not helping us. I had realized that being Brian's wife meant being his sole advocate, his protector, even though that role felt foreign, the shoes too big to fill.

I had big plans for the next day. Cheryl and Harold were going to help me get Brian in the car, and I was going to get him seen by someone qualified at the hospital if I had to scream at the top of my lungs to be heard. But you know what they say about making plans—God must have had a good laugh that day.

When Cheryl and Harold arrived, it became almost instantly clear that we couldn't get Brian into the car. In fact, we couldn't move him at all. The pain was too excruciating for him, and he couldn't move enough to help us progress so much as an inch. With shaking hands, I called 9-1-1 for an ambulance. Sirens were already blaring in my head as I waited for the sound of help on its way. I focused on putting Brian's shoes on his feet.

"I'm not going to the hospital," Brian said.

I held back what I'm sure would have been hysterical laughter. "Yes, you are."

"Well, I don't need an ambulance. I can get there myself."

"Brian," I whispered, leaning close to his face, "you can't even get to the *bathroom* by yourself." I regretted saying it almost instantly after the words left my mouth, but I set my face in what I hoped was an expression of compassionate resolution. Either because I had inadvertently shamed him or because he knew in his heart I was right, Brian acquiesced.

The ambulance arrived and the paramedics strapped Brian to a board. I almost let myself ask the question that had been plaguing me for weeks—*Is this really happening?*—but I pushed that thought down as I rode along in the back of the ambulance. I rattled off as much of Brian's medical history as I knew and, though I couldn't see outside from where I was sitting, I sent up a silent prayer that we'd be able to move faster, faster, faster. If there was ever a good time to speed, this seemed like it. I barely had time to stop, let alone stop and think; it felt like the road, the driver—the whole world—should be responding to the urgency of what was unfolding.

I was amazed to feel relief when I saw a familiar face behind the curtain around Brian's bed. It was the same doctor we had seen on that first visit to the Urgent Care Center. I was struck by how long ago that day seemed.

"I'm Dr. Goldstein—I remember you from right after Christmas." We shook hands. Brian seemed to be sleeping on the bed, but he stirred at the sound of my voice. Doctor Goldstein pressed on, talking to me with a certain intense directness that made me nervous. "Mrs. Howell, we've done some blood tests here, and you'll notice your husband is rather incoherent … Brian here is in acute renal failure, Mrs. Howell. I've called for an emergency transfer to Hillside Medical."

"Renal fail—? Hillside Medical is twenty-five minutes away. Why can't you do anything here? Is he so bad that you can't just help him *here*?" I was inexplicably attached to the idea that if Brian could be treated at the local ER, whatever was happening would stop happening. We'd stay close to home, close enough to get back to our lives without fighting traffic from Tulsa. It seemed like an important thing just then, to get home.

"I'm sorry, Mrs. Howell, we can't do anything for him here. We're just not equipped. But we've put in a catheter and we're gonna get him loaded up in the ambulance again."

The next hours whirled past in a weird dance of activity and stillness. Dance—follow the flashing lights and screaming sirens of the ambulance in front of me; stop—sign endless papers hanging from a dozen different clipboards. Dance—squeeze into the elevator next to Brian, who was only intermittently conscious of the tubes and machines attached to him and his gurney; stop—get a room on the sixth floor, struggle to comprehend why we're here in the ICU. Dance—more paperwork, so much that I convinced myself that the secret to Brian's wellness was hidden in lines of small, tightly-packed print; stop—words that sound mysteriously like "leukemia" and "lymphoma."

Then, seemingly without warning, there was no more dancing.

There was no more stillness.

There was just cancer.

Chapter
Six

I couldn't for the life of me remember who gave us the waffle iron.

I was sure it had been a gift—for our wedding, maybe, or a Christmas gone by—but as I stood there staring at it, waiting for the high-pitched chirp that signaled the end of the cooking cycle, I just couldn't remember who had given us the waffle iron.

Lately I had become a master of remembering, but it had taken me awhile to get there. Almost as soon as Brian was admitted to the hospital, I started writing things down; I didn't trust myself to get everything right every time I was asked to produce information—and I was being asked for information *a lot*. I knew I had to keep track of everything for Brian, who couldn't seem to regain lucidity after we transferred to Hillside; in fact, his delusions worsened. "The nurses are trying to kill me!" he'd whisper, holding me close to him in a vice grip. Then, seconds later, his head would loll sleepily to one side and he'd rouse himself to ask me the single question that seemed to plague him: "Do I have cancer?"

Cheryl and I told him time and again, "Yes, Brian, yes you have cancer. You're okay, Brian, you have cancer but we're here and you're okay ..." Each time we hoped the meaning of it would stick, that we wouldn't have to break the bad news yet again. We prayed for Brian to regain his clarity, the acuity and assuredness that was so much a part of who he was. Improvement would be slow, the oncologist told me, because whatever type of cancer Brian had was already in his spine.

In the meantime, I vowed to become Brian's memory.

Eventually, I came to remember everything: blood panel results from the previous day, the time and dosage of Brian's last round of pain medicine, the names of nurses and transport technicians, the schedule of lunch specials in the cafeteria, when our bills were due, our insurance information, Brian's medical history—both the lifelong trajectory of his wellness and the tumultuous, horrifying developments of the past month.

The beginning was the hardest. After the whirlwind at the end of January, it seemed like progress slowed to a slow-motion crawl.

"We've got to be sure about what it is before we try to treat it, Hayley … I'm sorry. I know 'hurry up and wait' is a tough pill to swallow, but if we treat for one and it's the other, we could do Brian more harm than good." Dr. Sanger had kind, light blue eyes set below a broad forehead and sandy blonde hair. He was the head of oncology at Hillside and my greatest ally in the fight against whatever was hurting Brian. Finding out the nature of the enemy—leukemia or lymphoma—was his primary focus during those first ten days in Tower Seven, the oncology floor at Hillside.

"I know, Doc, it's just—"

"I know. I really know. And what we don't know? We'll know soon."

And we did.

By February 10th—two weeks after Brian was admitted and exactly three years since the happy night when Brian and I got engaged—we knew what disease was ravaging Brian's body. On the list of details I remembered for Brian, this would be the most important. This would name the unnamable thing, unmask the bandit robbing our lives of normalcy: Burkitt's Lymphoma. The disease had already advanced to the fourth of four possible stages of severity. Brian's first round of chemotherapy began.

I remembered—seemed unable to forget—every morsel of information about Burkitt's I had been told or gathered myself since the diagnosis. The basic facts had become something of a mantra, one I repeated time and again as I tried to explain how Brian, seemingly in perfect health one day, became critically ill the next: *Burkitt's is an extremely rare, aggressive form of cancer. Only about 100-300 new cases appear in the United States each year, and plenty of those cases end in remission. Burkitt's is a kind of Non-Hodgkin's Lymphoma, which means the cancer comes from malignant B-cells. The cause of Burkitt's is unknown.*

But who gave us the waffle iron?

I wanted to remember so I could thank whoever it was—waffles with peanut butter and syrup had become one of the few things I could get Brian to eat since we had gotten home. And since he had lost 138 lbs. during his 38-day hospital stay, what Brian ate was one of my primary concerns.

Other concerns were keeping up with the mortgage, paying our bills and wrangling with the insurance company. Once a week had passed in the hospital and it became painfully clear that Brian wouldn't be going back to work any time soon, I was determined to keep us afloat no matter what it took. I called the Social Security office, our insurance company, got an FMLA from Brian's job ... but what no one at the electric company or the bank seemed to understand was that my husband had always been the one to take care of things, and now he wasn't even coherent enough to sign a check. Nothing was in my name, and regardless of how many times I explained our circumstances, I got shut out. To make matters worse, Brian's bosses terminated his employment in the second week of March. Their hearts were in the right place, because they got him inside a deadline for a government program that let him keep his insurance, but I was dreading delivering the news just the same. My fear of losing the house was immediate and pressing; there was no way to refinance our loan with Brian unable to make an appearance at the bank, and my salary wasn't enough to make quickly fraying ends meet.

One afternoon, Brian's brother, Steven, asked to speak with me in the hall outside Brian's room. Steve had been such a comfort to all of us since Brian got sick; he had a knack for explaining things simply for all of us. His doctorate degree in pharmacy made him especially able to understand the endless barrage of medical terms, procedures, and drug names that were quickly becoming part of our everyday vernacular.

"How you doing?"

"I'll be okay when Brian's okay," I answered quickly. It was the stock answer that had started jumping off my tongue every time someone asked me that question. It wasn't meant as a barb or anything—just as God's honest truth.

"Look, I spoke with Stephanie and … Hayley, we want to pay the mortgage on the house until Brian's back on his feet."

Emotions washed over me like a tidal wave: forceful and all-encompassing. Relief. Gratitude. And I can admit as much—shame. On the one hand, Steven was handing me a solution to my most pressing problem. On the other, I was overcome by how quickly Brian and I had lost our independence, how hurt Brian's pride would be if he found out we couldn't make it on our own. Brian and I shared a take-no-handouts philosophy; the truck was almost paid off, we were getting ourselves out of debt, and we had done it all by our own sweat and tears. It had only taken a month for us to fall behind.

Humbled. That feeling was there, too. Right then, I understood why "God opposes the proud but gives grace to the humble." When there is no pride left to cling to, there's plenty of room for grace.

"Thank you," I said, and I couldn't keep the tears from springing to the corners of my eyes. "This is … unbelievably helpful. Thank you."

"It's the least we can do, Hayls. And mom wants to help, too. She said she's depositing $500 into Brian's account today . You know, for bills and stuff."

"Wow, I—" I stuttered, practically speechless. "Thank you. Please thank Stephanie for me, too. But Steve?"

"Yeah?"

"I know Brian's been in and out and all, but even when he's 'in,' let's not tell him about this just yet. Okay?"

I didn't need to explain anything to Steven—he was Brian's brother, after all, and knew him as well as any brother should. Brian worked his butt off to earn what he had obtained, and what little pride he allowed himself came from that. *He's still going to have all of his possessions and his good name when he gets out of here*, I vowed to myself. I didn't know how I'd make it happen, I just knew I couldn't fail.

Even without the pressure of our mortgage and bills on my shoulders, I still felt the burden of carrying too much. Almost as soon as we had gotten to Tower Seven, I realized I had to act as Brian's primary caregiver regardless of how many doctors or nurses there were on staff. I was convinced I could offer Brian better care at home, and I knew instinctively that he'd heal with enough time in his own house, his own bed. But Brian still couldn't move on his own—a side effect of the chemotherapy and other drugs he had been given was neuropathy in his feet and legs, a condition that made any exertion painful and difficult. Doctor Sanger wouldn't budge on Brian's discharge given his physical condition, even after he finally emerged from the mental fog he'd been in since late January. By then—the end of March—Brian had become practically obsessed with the idea of puzzling out how his cancer came to be.

"It's not like that, babe," I explained. "They don't know what causes Burkitt's—"

"Well it has to be *some*thing," Brian said. I could tell by the resolve in his eyes that I was in for another lecture about a theory Brian held dear. "Everything causes cancer—we *know* that. What *they* won't tell you is that *they* already have the cure. Bet they've had it for a while. But they want money from cigarette companies and drug companies—so they keep us all on the hook."

"Babe, I—"

"No, listen. What if it's the benzene? You know? Or what if it's something else in the gas?"

Though I didn't want to encourage Brian, I'd also thought of the nights he'd come home reeking of gas after being practically drenched in the stuff at work. I thought of the way the sharp, distinct smell of it would sometimes seep through his pores long after he'd showered and changed into clean clothes. Part of me knew we were grasping at straws—we would have grasped at anything that brought a sense of logic or order to the chaos we felt raging all around us. But when Brian brought up his benzene theory to Dr. Sanger, he dismissed the idea like it was the musing of a child. And when I asked Dr. Sanger about the relationship between Burkitt's and the Epstein Barr virus—a virus Brian never had—he waved me off.

"I know you're looking at all this stuff on the Internet," he'd say, "but the Internet doesn't have an M.D."

And neither do you, I could almost hear him thinking. But Dr. Sanger was a good man. I'm sure a part of him understood how doubly devastating it is to cope with a diagnosis that doesn't seem to have a cause.

"How about this," he continued. "You keep a running tab of your questions in that notebook of yours, and I'll do my best to answer as many as I can, as best I can."

"So you've noticed my notebooks, huh?"

"I'm not the only one. The nurses here and on every other floor know about Hayley Howell. They know about her notebooks, and that she's always got questions, and about how she's taking vigilant care of her husband." He paused, taking in the embarrassment that must have shown on my face. His voice was softer when he continued. "They know you're doing exactly what they'd be doing if they were in your shoes."

In the beginning, my journals were just vague recordings of what Brian did each day. *February 6th—Brian tried to pull out his catheter today.* But lately the journals had transformed into something totally different. I continued to detail Brian's treatment and progress meticulously, but I also found more personal reflections spilling over onto page after page. For everyone else—Cheryl, Harold, Steven, the doctors and nurses, and of course, Brian—I put on a brave face. I focused on being as proactive as a person with her hands tied could be. But on the pages of my journals, the truth poured out like water, unstoppable and swift. It was only between the covers of a notebook that I could really admit how scared I was, how alone I felt. Sometimes, after filling ten pages in a sitting, I'd find myself surprised that everything I had written hadn't made the notebook impossibly heavy.

After what seemed like an eternity, Brian's second round of chemo ended. There were complications. Brian developed a fever that left him prone to infections, and the white cell count in his blood was dangerously low. I was sitting by Brian's bed one morning when a nurse came in to take his vitals. "Do you feel that?" she asked, her plump fingers pressed into the inner edge of Brian's wrist.

"Yeah, I guess I do," Brian said.

"Babe? What is—"

But before I could finish my sentence, nurses and doctors flooded into the room and rapid-fire chatter filled the air.

"What's happening?" I asked the pair of scrubs closest to me. I didn't recognize the face hovering above the too-familiar blue t-shirt.

"His heart rate's too high—around 200 beats per minute, actually. We need you to step outside, ma'am."

Suddenly I found myself in the hallway, staring at a closed door. I called Steven.

"Hayley, stay out of that room," Steven said.

"I am—but why? Steve, what are they doing in there?"

"They have to give him medicine that—well, look, it's like—imagine you have a car driving down a hill, and suddenly the brakes go out. You wouldn't be able to stop that car nice and slow, right? You'd have to put something in front of it—"

"Are you telling me they're crashing Brian's heart? That doesn't make sense, Steve. Just tell me what they're—"

"Hayley, they're gonna give him medicine that stops his heart cold. Then when it starts up again, it'll beat normally."

"Stop his heart? Like, *stop his heart*? Like they're in there killing my husband?"

"It's just for a second, Hayley, and they're not killing him—"

"Gotta go. I'll call you after. Better yet—"

"Already on my way."

Fifteen minutes later the same nurse who had led me out guided me back inside. Brian looked pale and a little stunned, but other than that he seemed okay.

"Whew," he exhaled a low whistle through his teeth. The faintest smile pulled at the corners of his mouth. "That was like being on a roller coaster!"

"I know, babe, I just talked to—"

"Best time I've had since I've been here!"

I gave Brian my widest smile and hoped he wouldn't notice the way my hands shook.

A few days later, after Brian had been fever-free for 48 hours and his blood panels showed improvement, Dr. Sanger told me I could take him home.

I knew Brian was nervous about leaving the hospital, even though both of us wanted to get out of room 7608 and never look back. "We got this," I reassured him, and I repeated the phrase to myself like a prayer. There was a lot to consider; shuttling Brian to and from the hospital and Dr. Sanger's office for tests and treatments would practically be a full-time job. Cleaning the house to align with hygienic precautions to keep Brian from getting sick would be another enormous undertaking. There were also the nuts and bolts of how Brian would get around our house. Between the walker, the wheelchair, the seat riser and the shower chair, though, I thought I had all our bases covered. The one adaptation I had refused were handrails. Imagining our walls lined with cold metal rails felt too much like turning our beloved home into just another hospital corridor. Burkitt's Lymphoma might be taking over our lives, but I wasn't about to let it take over the homestead.

Standing in the kitchen, slathering a hot waffle in peanut butter just three days after Brian was discharged, I felt the briefest glimmer of satisfaction that I had kept my promise so far. There I was, making my husband his favorite food and pouring him a big glass of chocolate milk to go alongside it, just like any other wife might for her husband. Maybe I would bring Brian his plate and he'd raise an eyebrow at the swing of my hips, or pull me onto his lap and kiss me hard on the mouth. Maybe one thing would lead to another and we'd get back to the business of making a baby, or maybe … maybe …

I didn't realize that I had started to cry until a hot, heavy tear splashed on the back of my hand. I choked on a sob and pressed my hand to my mouth; crying all over Brian's waffles seemed as serious a violation of my "stay positive in front of Brian" rule as crying right on his shoulder. But the truth that had hit me so hard in that moment was that we weren't just any other married couple. We were us. I was making Brian waffles with peanut butter and syrup because he needed to put on weight before he could begin his third round of chemo. I was pouring him a glass of thick chocolate milk because it was the only way he could get down the dozens of pills he had to take. And far from making babies, the only business we had together was fighting the disease that was trying so hard to tear us apart.

Chapter
Seven

April 30, 2010. A Short Story: My name is Hayley Howell and my husband's name is Brian. I am 28 and he is 35. We live in Owasso, OK, and two weeks ago we celebrated our two-year wedding anniversary. Before all this started, we were loving life, each other, our families. Everything was great.

I stared at the blinking cursor and the blank space after it. All that white, just begging to be tattooed with the details of what had happened to me and Brian in the past four months. I had come to realize it was exhausting to recount the details of our day-to-day lives with various members of the family and close friends each evening, and it was unspeakably painful to tell the story from its beginning to those who called out of the blue to play an innocent game of catch-up. I knew I had to find a way to keep everybody in the loop without risking my sanity, and one day the idea hit me like a lightning strike: Facebook. I settled in to compose my first "note" while Brian napped. It had been a hectic morning . . .

Today Brian went to the doctor and we didn't know they were going to do his spinal chemo today. We have learned to take the wheelchair Brian's parents got him because it's so much more comfortable than the ones in the office. So I wheeled him up to a tall recliner and he got in. Doctor Sanger came over to let us know Brian's PET scan and bone marrow biopsy looked good—whew! There was a small spot on Brian's jaw, which might be why his chin is numb, but the biopsy showed no signs of cancer and we are praising God for that!

Of course that doesn't mean we can stop the chemo. Brian will still receive eight rounds total, but Dr. Sanger said the next one should be easier than the last.

All of a sudden Brian said, "I don't feel so good." He went ghost white and seemed to be pouring sweat. The doctor called a nurse over just as Brian started looking like he was going to faint. His vitals were very low, and Brian was rushed to a recliner where he was hooked up to a liter of IV fluids. I held a cool washcloth to his forehead, and soon he was feeling much better.

I asked Dr. Sanger what protocol Brian is on. He said "Hyper CVAD," which I need to look up because I haven't heard of that from the other Lymphoma specialists I have talked to. He also gets Rituxan and Methotrexate—common lingo in our house now, I'm afraid. I have been educating myself about Burkitt's and its many treatments, or "protocols." We've been talking to other Lymphoma patients, too—it gets to be a kind of family in the chemo room.

Anyway, Brian asked the doctor about having fresh veggies and fruit, mainly because he's concerned about lettuce. For some of you who don't know, Brian is very prone to infections right now and can't have uncooked foods. I have had to be tough on this issue because Brian wants homemade tacos so bad! But Dr. Sanger said Brian's counts are up so that was a green light on lettuce. We stopped at Taco Bueno on the way home, and Brian was so glad to eat that lettuce! It's the small things in life we get a kick out of now.

So many of you have asked how you can help Brian, and we so appreciate that! First and foremost, your prayers are very precious and we feel them! We also love your cards. We read every single one of them, and they truly help us get through those boring, lonely hours at the hospital. It's hard not being able to see all of you and laugh with you and hear about your lives, but keep those cards comin' because we depend on them for support (and entertainment!).

Finally, details for the fund at Arvest Bank can be found below. As many of you know, I was unable to keep my job because caring for Brian is a full-time appointment, and of course Brian has not been working since January. Your donations help us with gas and food, especially when we have to spend long stretches at the hospital. THANK YOU to those who have donated—God works through your hands and makes anything possible.

I try to consider how many pages I filled with a story that cannot be contained by any number of words on any number of pages. The story—our story—has become something bigger than me, bigger than Brian, bigger than the big blue sky.

I find myself suddenly enthralled by the delicate gradations of blue outside my window. First there's just the faintest suggestion of color on top of the white clouds, then the pigment deepens through a series of blues so bold and brilliant I almost can't stand it. And just before the blue becomes too much to handle, all the bright turns dull and dark, until you're looking at the richest shade of navy you've ever seen. The top of the sky, as far as I can see, is like an endless bolt of velvet.

I remember feeling elated the day after I started posting on Facebook. It was such a strange feeling, happiness. That morning I had opened my email to find notification after notification of responses to my post. There was a flood of support from people we knew, total strangers, and everyone in between; and most importantly, there was an outpouring of prayer and well wishes from Burkitt's survivors. Theirs were the comments I clung to most, for reasons I'm sure I don't have to explain.

I remember the stark contrast of Brian's mood with my own. He was so melancholy, which was a surprise because he had been in pretty good spirits the day before. He sat in the plush lounger in the living room while I sprawled out on the couch with our laptop, planning my next post.

"Hayley?" he said.

"Yeah, babe?"

"I think this is gonna take me."

Just the memory of those words stab through my heart like a dagger, and in that moment I thought I could actually hear the sound of my soul shattering into a million little pieces. I drew a breath to start my objections, but stopped myself from talking when I saw the way Brian's face was set and grim. There was a certain serenity in his expression that made me wonder if he knew something I didn't. Silently, I followed his gaze out the bay window to the elm tree on our front lawn. The branches had just sprung to life again after a long winter made harder by the suffering we did in the cold months. Soon the canopy would be lush and full.

My voice sounded soft and far away when I spoke. "When the leaves change again, you're going to be a survivor."

May 26, 2010. Today they de-accessed Brian's port because he's done with round three of chemo. His vitals were good, except his blood pressure was low and his heart rate was high. Dr. S said that means Brian is low on fluids, so it was back to the treatment room to re-access the port.

Brian has lost ten pounds, which is not good. He'll be back to taking Megace, which is a medicine that's supposed to make you hungry. That means we'll be leaving extra time in the mornings for McDonald's breakfast on our way to appointments!

We met two nice ladies in the treatment room. Cindy was diagnosed with Stage 3 colon cancer and has had 11 of 12 rounds of chemo. She looked great for what she's been through, and said she will start praying for Brian. The lady on our other side was much older and also had colon cancer, which she has been fighting for three years now. Brian told them his story and they couldn't believe he used to be close to 300 lbs. I had to show them a picture to prove it!

June 4, 2010. Today as we sat in the doctor's office for treatment, I noticed that Brian's eyebrows are almost all gone now. He looks like a cancer patient. I guess I never noticed the physical effects of the chemo before because we're always so focused on numbers, numbers, numbers. Hemoglobin, temperature, blood pressure, heart rate, white blood cell count (so important!), and platelets. But his eyelashes are thinning out, too, and those big baby blues and I are gonna be mighty sad to see them go.

We got to the moment of truth … the scale … (drum roll, please) … Brian gained 13 pounds! The nurse said she was so proud of Brian, and he was proud of himself, too.

Cytology on the spinal fluid came back … negative! That means no cancer in the spinal fluid—PRAISE GOD!

Dr. Sanger looked at the spot on Brian's back, which has doubled in size. He said it doesn't feel like a tumor, but is probably a cyst. We have to keep an eye on it, but I feel much better knowing it's not a tumor.

Brian took the words right out of my mouth in the car: "Well this was a good appointment!" It really was. On the way home we drove down Cherry Street to see what food options Brian will have when he's in the hospital next week. There was a Chimi's and a Jason's Deli and a Whataburger ... oh, the possibilities!

We'll check in Monday and stay until Saturday or Sunday. To be honest with all of you, being in the hospital is starting to wear on Brian and me both—visitors during visiting hours are greatly encouraged!

June 16, 2010. The other day Brian and I were sitting in Dr. Sanger's office when a woman walked by wearing a bright pink shirt that read SURVIVOR under a big, darker pink ribbon. Later we saw the same woman in a recliner getting treatment.

"She's not a survivor," Brian said to me. I shushed him because I didn't want her to hear—you all know Brian, he doesn't care much what people think. But I said, "What do you mean she's not a survivor? She's obviously got breast cancer and she's fighting it."

"Exactly," Brian said to me. "She's fighting it. How can you be a survivor if you're still fighting?"

So I went to the t-shirt shop yesterday and got Brian a blue t-shirt. I had a neon green ribbon and "FIGHTER ... soon to be SURVIVOR" screened right onto the front. I thought it was perfect, but then I had another idea—so I had "Burkitt's Lymphoma SUCKS" printed on the back in smaller letters that will sit between Brian's shoulder blades.

Well today I gave Brian the shirt when he was getting ready to go and he loved it! I'm having another one made in a button-down so he can have his port accessed without changing into a gown or stretching the neck on his t-shirts.

I couldn't resist—I got one for me, too. It's true after all—we are fighting together and with God's grace we will be a husband and wife who SURVIVED this terrible disease and the difficult treatment it takes to beat it.

June 29, 2010. Now that Brian has finished up round 4 of his chemo, Dr. Sanger wanted him to have the cyst on his back removed before we start round 5. Brian's white blood cell count is very good right now and he's feeling strong, so there will hopefully be less of a chance of infection if we get the cyst removed now and Brian gets a week to recover before the next bout of chemo knocks his counts down again. So today we went to see Dr. Jones, the surgeon who did Brian's lymph node biopsy back in late January when all this started. He remembered Brian, but Brian couldn't remember him. "Yeah," said Dr. J, "you were kinda out of it then."

He numbed Brian up and then I watched when he pulled out the sac and cleaned up all the pus—there was a lot of that stuff! I guess I have a strong stomach for this kind of thing because I found it fascinating. "You should think about going to nursing school"—that's what a lot of people have said when they see me care for Brian. But I think it's different when you care for the person you love most in the world. Nothing about my best friend, my soul mate, could ever disgust me or make me love him less, but I'm not sure I'd want to see some stranger's cyst get removed! LOL!

Please keep praying for Brian, and thank you for your donations to his fund! If you're interested in donating, please find details below.

Now, sitting in a plane thousands of miles above the ground, I am overcome by the list of things I never wrote about. While so much of our story has been made public—because I have made it so, or tried to—there are precious few details that I have kept for my memory alone.

I never wrote about my hair falling out in big clumps, or the forty pounds I lost just from worrying so darn much. I never wrote about the surgical mask I forced myself to wear to bed each night, or the way I started to fear getting too close to my own husband. I never wrote about "The Incident."

At the time it seemed irreverent to write about moments when Brian wasn't exactly a peach; after all, the man had *cancer.* There's a certain earthly sainthood that gets conferred on cancer patients, I think, and for plenty of good reasons. But up here, the dark velvet sky invites my secrets, and I think it might feel good to confess to the vast stretches of pure blue.

The Incident began when Harold and Cheryl let me know that they'd be bringing over a pork loin with Brian's favorite—Dink's barbeque sauce—for dinner. I was always happy to have home-cooked food brought to us since I didn't have time to do much cooking myself, and Brian had been the primary gourmand in our house before he got sick. The process of having company over, though, was slightly complicated due to the sanitation requirements we all had to uphold: removing shoes, disinfecting anything brought in the house from the outside, compulsive hand-washing. But the three of us had devised a kind of assembly line to streamline our entrance. Harold pulled bags out of the car, Cheryl ferried them up the front walk, and I brought it all from the door to the kitchen sink, where everything got sprayed down with diluted bleach.

The three of us had struck up such a rhythm—carry, drop, repeat; carry, drop, repeat—that I was taken completely by surprise when a cluster of bags was heavier than all the previous ones together. The bag in the center slipped right out of my hand, and somehow managed to gain a bit of swinging momentum as I turned. I ended up lobbing it a foot or two, and then—

"What was *that*?" Brian asked from his recliner.

He had heard the sharp *crack* of glass breaking as the bag hit the floor.

"It was ..." I hesitated, but I knew I was just delaying the inevitable. "It was the barbeque sauce. But I can probably salvage it!"

Only I couldn't. The bottle had shattered into a million pieces, and even if I could have found a way to separate the minute shards from the thick sauce, the germs on the outside of the bottle would have already contaminated what was inside.

Brian gathered up all his energy to bellow out his reprimand. "What are we supposed to do now?" he yelled. "That's the *only* thing I was looking forward to—the only thing!"

"Brian, I'm sorry, really sorry, babe. I can go get you—"

"No! It has to be Dink's. Anything else isn't worth eating."

Harold and Cheryl could see how terrible I felt, and they both graciously scrambled to take the blame. "I should have told you that was a heavy one," Cheryl offered, and Harold said he'd be willing to drive the 45 minutes in both directions to go back to Dink's and renew our sauce stash.

"No, thank you, but no—you can't do all that driving now, it's too late. We'll just have to make do with something else, and I'm sure it'll be delicious," I rambled. I felt so inexplicably guilty—it was an honest mistake, after all—and my instinct was to busy myself rather than give in to feeling bad.

"I can't believe you did this," Brian grumbled.

My guilt was on the verge of becoming something far more defensive and fierce. "Brian, I obviously made a *mistake*," I said as gently as I could. "We're doing our best—mistakes happen."

I could see the look in Brian's eyes flutter between irritation and forgiveness. In that moment he settled on the latter, but he never let me live it down. When he was finally well enough to be in public, he had me take him to the grocery store to pick out his own barbeque sauce. Clearly, it was an errand with which I couldn't be trusted.

I catch a glimpse of my reflection in the small, oval-shaped airplane window and silently chastise myself in Brian's voice. *"You gotta be more careful, babe."* And just like every other happy memory that sets my heart on fire, here comes the inevitable backlash of sadness. Now a different kind of heat—one that burns in the back of my throat and behind my eyes—starts to take over. *Ah, velvet sky,* I think, *why did you make me tell?*

Chapter Eight

No one was around to see the fire start.

Had the little town of Canadian, Oklahoma not been experiencing a water main problem, or had most of the town not been evacuated to a nearby hotel because of it, someone might have had eyes on the piece of the landscape where my mother's house was sitting. They might have sent up the alarm in time to save the structure or the possessions it sheltered, or at least call the fire department. But no one was around to see the fire start. So it burned.

Brian and I were in Dr. Jones' office to have his cyst site checked out and repacked when I got the call. At first I thought it was a joke—though why anyone would go out of their way to tell such a bad one should have occurred to me immediately. It was the pictures my mom sent that helped the truth sink in like a rock dropping to the bottom of a still lake; the plot was charred and black, with only the grill and a brick stairwell left to mark the place where the house had once stood. No one was hurt, which I felt utterly blessed about, and all our family memorabilia had actually been housed somewhere else for years—another blessing—but all the necessities for day-to-day living were gone.

The next morning, I set out early to make the 90-minute drive to my mom's. Cheryl had come to our house early to spend time with Brian, and I made good time on the highway. I had barely pulled up to the house—or rather, the spot where the house used to be—when I got a call from Brian.

"Hey, babe, what's up?"

"I just got a call from Judi," Brian said. Judi was Dr. Schaffer's RN, and one of the most supportive, helpful people Brian and I had met during the past seven months. "She says they got the results from my PET scan and now they want me to have an MRI."

"Why? What'd they see?" For the second time in as many days, I had that feeling like a stone was dropping from a skyscraper down to the pit of my belly. Friends of ours—people we had connected with after I found a network of Burkitt's patients and survivors—had told us that their doctor had called for an MRI after a PET scan "lit up like a Christmas tree." Bright spots against the dark, smoky base of the scan only meant one thing.

"Well, she says they saw some spots on my brain and—"

"Give me 90 minutes. I'll meet you at the hospital."

And I did. My mom understood, of course. "You being here can't un-burn the house," she said. We hugged for a long time before I got back in the car.

Despite his worry over the pending MRI results, Brian was in good spirits that night and the next day.

"Babe?"

"Yes, Brian?" I said over the top edge of my computer. I was using a little afternoon downtime to write another Facebook note covering the events of the last several days. Just then, I had decided to erase everything about the fire at my mom's; the firefighters suspected an electrical malfunction from an air conditioner caused the spark, and I thought it best to avoid the subject publicly in case things got ... *legal*.

"You know we missed our wedding anniversary this year."

"Yeah, well, we were a little busy, babe."

There was gentleness in his voice when Brian continued. "Well, I'm not busy now, and I'd like to take my wife out on a date tonight."

"Really? You feel—"

"I feel like I want to take my beautiful wife to dinner."

The idea of it was so exquisite, I found myself at a loss for words.

That night, we ate at the Mexican restaurant Brian and I always went to for special occasions. We laughed and talked and drank over large glasses of sweet tea, and for a few hours it felt like we could both see the light at the end of the long, dark tunnel we'd been walking through all those months.

The next day, Brian and I were back in the hospital to get the MRI results. Doctor Schaffer explained that the MRI revealed a spot on Brian's brain—and he took care to explain the difference between a spot *on* versus *in*. Whatever Brian had—and they'd have to perform a biopsy to find out, because it could just be inflammation or it could be a tumor—it was *on* the brain, nestled between Brian's skull and the brain itself. The whole scenario was complicated by the fact that Brian's counts were low again. His white blood cells were having trouble bouncing back after the fourth round of chemotherapy, so the fifth couldn't start up until those counts were up to better levels.

"What's the plan?" I asked Dr. Schaffer.

"Always plan-focused, Hayley, that's a good thing," he began. "The plan is to hurry up and wait until next week, when we re-check the counts to see if Brian can start Round 5 of his chemo and get that spot on his brain biopsied."

"We got this," I said, as much to Brian as myself.

"I know you do," said Dr. Schaffer. I felt suspicious of the silent worry behind his small smile, but said nothing about it to Brian.

July 12, 2010. Today Brian and I left to go to his appointment at Dr. S's to check his labs and make sure his white count is at least a 4.0 so he can start treatment today. I got the car packed with all the usual stuff: socks and undies, sanitation wipes, pop-up air fresheners, wafer cookies (chocolate and strawberry are Brian's favorites!), king size peanut butter cups, root beer, and a fresh package of Nutter Butters.

They did the blood draw and we sat down to wait. Eventually, one of our favorite nurses came over and asked if we had gotten our results—we hadn't, I told her. So she waved me over to the computer after pressing a few buttons. I knew from the look on her face it wasn't great. Brian's white count had actually dropped since last week, from 0.5 to 0.3. The nurse went to tell Judi and came back with a mask for Brian, too — he can't be getting sick with so few white blood cells to fight off any infections.

When Judi came over I didn't like the look on her face. She said that Brian will have to have a bone marrow biopsy. Brian asked her what she thought was going on? Judi said it's either 1) the bone marrow's just not producing or 2) the chemo knocked the bone marrow really far down. She says she hopes it's the latter of the two, since that way they'll be able to harvest Brian's own bone marrow and use it for the bone marrow transplant.

The ride home was not a fun one as you might guess. "What ifs" are running rampant in our minds: What if Brian has to find a bone marrow match for a transplant? What if we have to go to Dallas to get it because our insurance won't cover a closer facility? What if? What if? What if?

Brian was worried about the brain biopsy and now he's doubly worried about the bone marrow biopsy. I try not to show him that I am worried, and I try to hide it from myself too, to keep myself from getting so depressed.

July 16, 2010. This past Thursday at around 4:30 p.m., one of our physical therapists came to the house to do an evaluation on Brian. When she walked into the bedroom, his leg started to twitch. "Are you doing this to yourself?" she asked Brian. He said no, so the PT told me to call our doctor and let him know what was going on. I spoke to Judi, who said in the most seriously urgent tone I've ever heard her use, "Hayley, you get him to the ER right now." Long story short, Brian had a focal seizure. It wasn't one of those shaking, foaming-at-the-mouth seizures you see on TV — thank God. Just the leg shaking and that was it. They gave us some new medicine and sent us home.

By this time it was 9:30 p.m. We went to the 24-hour pharmacy to get his prescription filled and stopped for a bite to eat. When we got home Brian was exhausted and headed straight to the bathroom to get ready for bed. I set out his nightly medications as usual. We were both so tired.

Brian was washing his hands and I was about to get his toothbrush ready but he said "No, babe, I'm just so tired I'm gonna go to bed." He started to walk out of the bathroom and stopped. "You okay, babe?" I asked. "I forgot how to walk," said Brian. I didn't understand what that meant but from the look on Brian's face I knew something wasn't right. I helped him over to the bed — I was half-dragging him—and then I said, "Do you think this is another seizure?" Brian took a breath to answer me and then BOOM—he went into total body convulsions. I was so scared. Brian's eyes were twitching and his whole body shook then stiffened up like a board. I grabbed the phone and managed to get Brian onto the floor, where I thought he'd be safest. All of a sudden the twitching stopped but Brian was unconscious. Breathing, I told the 9-1-1 operator, but unconscious.

The woman on the phone talked me through putting the animals away, opening the front door, turning on all the lights … I kept running back to the bedroom to look at Brian, call his name. By the time the paramedics got there— and they were there quick—Brian was breathing heavy and drooling a bit. I gave the EMTs the A-B-C version of what's been going on the past seven months and made sure they knew Brian is neutropenic and all of that.

I called Cheryl from the car and she called Steve. I called my mom, too. We all met up at the hospital.

By then Brian was coherent again, but he didn't know what day it was. He kept asking me, but he was confused because we had just been in the ER earlier in the day and he thought he had been home for much longer than the 30 minutes we were there.

After all night in the ER, Brian is in a room in the ICU on the 5th floor. He will be there all weekend and we don't know when he'll be able to come home. To make matters worse, Dr. S is on vacation next week.

This ICU isn't like the one in Tower 7. Here they are strict about their "policies." There is no sleeping in the room with patients and they kick you out from 6:30-8:00 a.m. because they are "closed." Well I don't care and I'm not leaving! My marriage isn't "closed" is it? Brian's cancer doesn't "close," does it?

I've been told that the seizures could be from an infection in the spinal fluid or the spot on his brain (if it's cancer cells and not just inflammation). Ruling out infection is goal #1. Our doctors have ordered a lumbar puncture and bone marrow biopsy. Both are scheduled for later today (because now it's Friday—yes, I've pretty much been up all night and yes, of course I'm tired but I can't sleep).

Antibiotics are the story for now. Brian is getting a strong pain medication too, which keeps him sleeping. His head is really hurting and so is his rib, where the PET scan and MRI showed a mass of cancer cells.

I am TERRIFIED. I do not want to lose my best friend, my soul mate, my world. I love him more than he could ever know … at times like these I shut down. I don't talk to anyone except Brian. I don't want to leave his side, and I pray more than anyone could ever imagine. After seven months of the unknown, seven months of treatments and hospitalizations and thinking things are getting better only to have them get much, much worse—to say we're tired … well, there just aren't words for how tired we are. But Brian and I are strong and we will make it through!

My request to all reading this: Please, please pray for Brian. If you go to church, please put him on your prayer list if you haven't already. Both Brian and I trust in the Lord and know that he walks with us every day. With God all things are possible!

July 17, 2010. Last night and this morning went fine. Steve came down and settled my nerves like he always does. Thank you, Steve!

Brian hasn't had any more seizures. The neurosurgeon said that the seizures were probably produced by a cancerous spot on the brain. He won't perform surgery until the WBC is up to a 2.0 or higher, but when he does the surgery he'll take out the whole mass (instead of just doing a biopsy first), and then radiation will be the next step to make sure there is nothing left in that spot.

Our substitute oncologist is putting Brian on Leukine, a medicine that will help the white blood cells grow. He's also been given Dilaudid, a strong pain reliever, because the bone marrow biopsy has left him very uncomfortable. The medicine knocks him out, so Brian didn't hear my conversation with the hospitalist about taking him home. I want to so badly—I know it's the best place for him to be, and I can care for him as well if not better than a nurse. He can eat his own food, see the doggers, and sleep in his own bed. And so can I!

Thank you all for your prayers and messages. God is good!

July 18, 2010. Brian had a mild focal seizure last night. The hospitalist and oncologist have decided we're here for at least a week, until WBC is 2.0 or higher. Even though Brian and I would rather be home, the seizures make me nervous because they come so quick.

Hopefully the Leukine injections will up the WBC so the neurosurgeon can come in and do his magic.

"Hurry up and wait" is the name of the game at this point ... no surprise there.

July 21, 2010. Brian is being discharged today with WBC up to 1.5!
A little while ago one of Dr. S's associates came in with the bone marrow biopsy results ... drum roll please ... CLEAN!!! PRAISE GOD!

July 22, 2010. Brian is feeling weak since the discharge but he did take a shower today, which was much needed and made him feel so much better! We got a call from the neurosurgeon, who said they are scheduling Brian for surgery on the 26th. We also had Brian's labs checked and his WBC is 2.7! Brian was in such a great mood, talking and laughing with everyone. He told Judi she was being needy when she was asking him how he was doing. She laughed. "Do you think that's why I'm not married?" she asked. "Yeah," said Brian, "you'd be a pretty good girlfriend for about a month, but then they'd get to know you." He was kidding of course and we love Judi—I was just so glad Brian was in good spirits.

Things are looking up again—white blood cell count is good, Brian is feeling good and we are praying he continues to be seizure-free. Thank you for following us on our journey and God bless!

The next day, the seizures resumed in full force. We were alone in the house when the first one came; I was helping Brian get through his physical therapy exercises when he suddenly felt funny.

"I'm really scared, Hayley," he said to me.

"Just relax, babe, it's just gonna be a little focal tremor and it will pass," I told him. Inside, terror licked at my heart like a hot flame against dry wood.

Seconds later, Brian bit himself so hard during his convulsions that his chin and lower jaw turned blue.

All the way to the hospital and through the night, the joy in my heart at Brian's good numbers and humor and supposed improvement was slowly turned to ash by the fear raging in my chest. I tried to fight it—tried to hang on to the shred of hope I had allowed myself to feel.

But we had been battling for so long and I was so tired, and it was all I could do to keep my tears from falling and drowning us all.

No one was around to see the fire start.

So it burned.

Chapter Nine

"**F**olks, we're just about ready to prepare for landing. We ask that you make your way to your seats and … listen for announcements from the flight crew about landing procedures. On behalf of everyone here at …"

I realize I've managed to doze for a few minutes—thirty or so—and wake to find Hank awake but bleary-eyed next to me. The sky outside is a kind of forever-blue.

"Morning," I say.

"And to you."

We smile the uncomfortable smile of strangers suddenly aware of how vulnerable they've been, sleeping next to one another like trusting children.

"How long do you have?"

"What's that now?" Hank asks.

"How long do you have—for your layover? You mentioned you're heading on to Colorado."

"Oh, right, Colorado. I guess I'll have about 45 minutes if we get in when we're supposed to."

"Oh."

The conversation withers and Hank mercifully makes "a last dash to the facilities."

I look down and realize I've been cradling an airline pillow, absentmindedly stroking the sterile coverlet in a motion my fingers are habituated to mimic. I miss the doggers already, though I only just left them this morning. Zoe, Chloe, and Libby—our little girls. I can feel the small smile that never quite blooms into a grin slide over my lips.

The day you brought Libby to the hospital.

Brian had been having a rough couple of days. He was practically through his 28-round cycle of radiation treatments, but the exhaustion was getting to him. I thought seeing our little chocolate wiener dog would cheer him up, and once I got it in my head to sneak Libby in … well, I was determined to see it done.

So I gave Libby a bath and cooed to the other dogs, who weren't happy about all the attention being lavished on their sister. I grabbed a bag of mine I knew Libby would fit in and we both piled into the truck "to see Daddy!" Of course, when I showed up at the hospital and tried to put Libby in the bag, she wouldn't have it. I grabbed Brian's blue fleece blanket—I had just had it home for washing—and wrapped that little dog up like a baby. I was nervous and practically shaking as I carried her through the halls, but I realized anyone I passed would probably just assume I was cradling a child. That's what women do in hospitals, isn't it? Walk their babies through the halls, whispering to the soft motion of footfall, footfall, footfall . . .

When I walked into Brian's room, out popped our little Libby.

"Babe," Brian said, a look of abject horror on his face, "why did you do that? We're gonna get into trouble!"

"No we're not," I said. "I wanted to put some sunshine in your day."

"Well, I have never been able to break the law and I'm not going to be able to relax with her here."

I couldn't help but laugh at his seriousness. "Always a stickler for the rules, huh?"

"You know I am," he said, but there was no playfulness in his eyes.

We left minutes later, after I snapped a photo of Brian and Libby: her big brown eyes studying her Daddy's face, his curious smell; his big blues, linked by a wrinkle of irritation and worry in his brow. I suppose it might seem cruel to people who didn't know Brian—that he would send me and Libby away after all the fussing we did to get to him. But that was Brian being Brian—and that's all I ever wanted.

"Almost got caught," Hank says, a little breathless as he buckles himself back into his seat.

"Hm?"

"Caught being up and about—that stewardess gave a look like I was breakin' Marshall Law or something." His warm smile is infectious.

"We wouldn't want that, now."

"No, ma'am, that we would not."

July 26, 2010. Surgery Day. The schedule for today: 10 a.m.—MRI. 2 p.m.—Surgery. Then to ICU for recovery and monitoring.

As of now, we're ahead of schedule. Transport came to take Brian for his MRI at 8:25, and when he came back 45 minutes later I gave him a sponge bath. By 10:20 he was in pre-op getting fluids, and soon after, the neurosurgeon came around and marked Brian's head with a "W." Brian said, "Let's get it on!" and the doctor said, "That's what I'm talking about!"

12:37 p.m.—They came to wheel him to the OR. I walked as far as I could with the gurney. I hate rushing our goodbyes, and I never really say "goodbye" either. I say, "I love you. See ya later."

The whole family came out to wait with me today: Cheryl and Harold, Steve and Stephanie with the kiddos, Brian's grandma, my mother, her brother and his wife, Brian's dad, and one of each of our cousins. The wait seemed like forever, but having everyone there praying was a great help. At 3:05 the neurosurgeon came out. He took me and Steve into the hallway to talk.

The mass wasn't encapsulated like they had hoped, and what that means is the malignant cells were pressed into Brian's brain. To sum it up, they did not get the whole tumor. The new plan is to wait 10-14 days for Brian to heal, then start radiation. Until then, there could be more seizures, but please join me in praying that does NOT happen.

When they told me I could go see Brian in the 6th floor ICU I could not move fast enough to get there! Steve and I told the family about the surgery, but we all think it is best not to mention to Brian that the entire tumor couldn't be removed. He needs to stay positive in order to get well, so for now we will just celebrate that the surgery went okay.

When I got upstairs I saw that Brian was set up in room 6309, directly across the hall from where all this began on January 27th—six months ago tomorrow. At first I was overwhelmed by the bad memories of that place; that was the room where we found out about Brian's cancer. But then I realized maybe this is us coming full circle, and maybe God is letting me know that soon it will be like we were never in that room, because soon we'll be survivors.

July 28, 2010. *The doctors have let us know that the 2-3 days after the surgery are the worst for swelling, so after tomorrow we should see a lot of improvement. Brian is very anxious about the "s-word"—I try to keep everything in perspective for him, but inside I am dreading any seizures, too.*

Last night our nurse was a cute girl. Brian has always said that petite girls are "cute"—and that I am not "cute," I am pretty. Anyway, once the nurse left I asked Brian, "Do you think she's cute?" He said: "Oh, I guess ... but not as cute as my wife." That just melted my heart! The love I feel for Brian is so powerful, so much more than love ... so I will end this "note" with a note: Cherish every moment you have! Trust in God! Pray for Brian!

June 29, 2010. *Today has been a long and stressful day. Brian has remained pretty much sedated because he is so anxious about having another "s-word." A radiation oncologist came by to talk to us about starting radiation therapy right away—so Monday, that will begin. She said they will treat the whole brain, not just the place where the cells were. The hospitalist also came by and said that Brian's WBC won't go down until the chemotherapy begins (it was up to 18.0 because of the medicines he was taking before the surgery). I said no, it would drop quickly now that he's not on the medicine. She told me I was wrong.*

When one of our nurses came by later, I asked her about the WBC results for the day.

2.5.

But what do I know? I'm only a wife.

Around mid-morning transport came to take Brian downstairs for some pre-radiation testing. I sat in a tiny waiting room where I could see Brian through a window the whole time! That was nice.

While I was waiting, I noticed a young man sitting nearby—a volunteer. Lately I am not one to chat with anyone, but this man was about Brian's age and when he asked me how I was doing, I smiled and said: "I'll be fine when my husband is fine," (as I always say). The young man told me that he was diagnosed with Hodgkins Lymphoma 10 years ago, and that his father had Non-Hodgkins Lymphoma, and they are both doing fine. I guess God knows that I need to hear those stories right now.

When we got back to Brian's room, I don't know how or why, but I just lost it. I try never to cry in front of Brian, but I was just so emotionally drained and so filled with all different emotions—sadness and hope and fear and yes, maybe the feeling of being a little depressed. I asked Brian if he wanted to talk about things and he said no. He saw my tears and asked me if I felt lonely. I nodded. I told him how much I love him.

That's when Brian's pumps started to beep-beep-beep like crazy.

A nurse came in and fixed the pumps, then asked Brian how he was doing. "I've been better," said Brian. "Well you've been worse, too," said our nurse. Then he looked at me and saw the tears running down my face. He didn't have to ask how I was doing. Instead he asked if we'd like to pray together. He said a very nice prayer, and told us he's seen people come back from a lot worse than what we are dealing with. "Have faith!" he said. I think Brian and I both needed to hear that.

Cheryl came by in the afternoon to relieve me. I told Brian I had to go take a shower. What I really need is sleep—I get so much more anxious when I don't sleep well. I cried the whole way home in the car; it's a safe place to let it out, I've realized.

I came back to find that Brian had been moved to the 4th floor, which I'm not happy about because the nurses here don't know us. They are slow and treat us like Joe Shmoes off the street. Brian's pump started beeping at 9:40 p.m. and it's now 10:16 as I write this and still no one has come in! Don't worry—I turned the pump off like I saw the nurse do earlier in the day. But seriously? Waiting this long is ridiculous!

So overall I, for one, did not have a good day. Brian didn't either. Please Lord, when will Brian be okay?

July 20, 2010. *PLEASE PRAY. We got news this morning that we didn't want. The cancer is now all throughout Brian's spine along with the brain from what the MRI shows. Radiation will happen and a bone marrow/stem cell transplant needs to happen, too. But we won't know any details until Monday, when Dr. S finally returns. Brian and I both feel like we've been in the ocean without a life preserver for two weeks now.*

The doctor that came in this morning (another Dr. S associate) said that Brian can't have the transplant until he is in remission. But they can't do chemo until after radiation. But they don't want to do radiation on the spine because that kills the bone marrow. "You're damned if you do, you're damned if you don't," he said. Between you and me, though, that doctor has never been too positive.

I really won't have any information until Monday. I have the worst feeling possible. Brian is scared that he's going to die. And we are both crying. WHY? Please dear Lord, have mercy on Brian! Please Lord, let us grow old together!

I told Brian that he has a lot of things to do here and that he has to survive. He still has to take me to Niagara Falls and to a baseball game and please, please grow old with me. Brian looked at me and said: "There is a good chance that won't happen." I could feel my heart breaking into a thousand pieces.

We have come too far to give up! Brian was doing so well before the seizures and now it feels like all our hard work is falling apart. I have asked all of you to pray before … I am really asking now. Brian is my best friend, my lover, my soul mate. I cannot live without him. Please, please, please pray.

That weekend I forced myself to go home. I needed to shower, sleep, and breathe air not tinged with the acrid smell of industrial-strength disinfectant. I needed to hug my dogs and eat food off of real plates.

I sat in Brian's recliner for a long time. I imagined my figure settling into a groove left by his body and leaned my head back into the place I imagined his broad shoulders would have been. I looked out the window to the old elm. *"When the leaves change again, you're going to be a survivor."* How long ago had I said the words with so much quiet power, so much surety? I wondered how they would taste in my mouth if I said them again, if I dared utter the promise that had become a question that had become a dim hope.

So I whispered.

Tentative and sweet, the sentence had the curious flavor of some exotic fruit, familiar but completely unique.

I said it again, louder, and felt myself celebrate the audacity of a taste so bold.

"When the leaves change again, you're going to be a survivor," I said aloud, and this time it had all the familiarity of a Granny Smith apple, green and ripe.

I gathered up my things and returned to Hillside.

August 2, 2010. This morning Dr. S came in! We were happy to see him but not so happy about what he had to tell us. Brian asked him if he is worse than when he first checked in back in January. "Not worse," Dr. S said, "just different. The cancer was in your bone marrow and all throughout your body in January. It is now in the bones but not in the marrow. And because it's Burkitt's, and Burkitt's is a blood cancer, those cancer cells are still all throughout the body—all of which we knew back in January."

He really didn't have anything much to add, other than letting us know the transplant doctors are going to do a consult with Brian to get that rolling. Steve will get tested to see if he is a match, but really the ideal situation is to use Brian's own stem cells or bone marrow so neither will be rejected.

I expressed worry that without chemo, the cancer in the spine will get worse and spread. Dr. S reminded me that the cancer is already metastatic, so that is not a worry we can address right now. And as far as chemo and radiation at the same time, the toxicity would be too great. "The negative would outweigh the positive," he said, and I know that what he really meant is that too much right now could kill Brian. That scared me.

Brian expressed his concerns, too, especially about being paralyzed on his right side still. He was doing great about 3 weeks ago with PT and OT, but his progress has stopped and now he's worse than before. Dr. S assured him that once the cancer is gone, his mobility will come back. That was a bright spot in all the cloudy news.

Brian got emotional when Dr. S was here. He told him that he trusts him with his life and hopes Dr. S can cure him.

I followed Dr. S into the hall and asked him if he is still optimistic. And he said yes, because we are not at a last resort yet. We have to do three things: radiation, chemo, and the transplant. Dr. S knows I like a plan and I think he knew I would take heart in thinking of Brian being better in 1-2-3 steps. We all know it is not that easy, but still . . .

When I went back inside, Brian and I had a talk. I told him he has to start thinking "Yes, I am going to be a survivor and yes, I am going to make it through this!" I reminded him of when we first started dating and he tried to break it off with me. "What did you say to me?" I asked him. "You said 'no one's ever fought for me before.' And I am STILL FIGHTING FOR YOU and always will, but you have to fight for you, too. If not for you, for me. Fight for me, and I'll fight for you, and together we'll beat this and go back to living our lives."

I have had a sense of peace come over me since the weekend, and I think Brian sensed that, too. I really do think God is working in me, and I feel sure that Brian IS going to be okay. I have to keep looking forward to him being healed. I have to do that for myself, so I can remain strong, and for Brian, so he will not get overcome by the way things are right now.

Please pray for Brian's body that he makes it through these 3 very long steps, and pray for Brian's mind and heart, so both can be strong enough to endure what it takes to become CANCER-FREE. God is good!

Chapter Ten

August 18, 2010. *Radiation is over! As many of you know, radiation was a very tiring sequence of treatments for Brian, so we are very glad that is over and done with.*

Now we move onto the R-ICE chemotherapy protocol, which will be given over a 3-4 day period. After the second round, Brian will have a scan to see how things are progressing.

Dr. S said that he'd like to use a donor for Brian's bone marrow transplant because the Burkitt's was in Brian's bone marrow in the beginning. I have mixed feelings about this; using Brian's own marrow, there is no risk of rejection but there is a risk of Burkitt's cells. Using a donor, there's no risk of Burkitt's but there is potential for rejection. It's a real catch-22.

The hospitalist came in today. The chest x-ray Brian had this morning showed pneumonia—fluid in the lower left lung. I have been asking various nurses to listen to Brian's lungs for DAYS because he sounds phlegmy to me. "No, everything sounds clear," they say after listening to him breathe for 2.5 seconds. Okay, I always tell myself, what do you know, Hayley? You're only a wife. Anyway, now Brian is on antibiotics and his breathing treatments have been increased now to every 6 hours while he's awake. Another alarming thing to worry about . . .

Brian's head looks like he has a sunburn and is peeling like he has one, too. This is an effect of the radiation. I wash his face and head with cool water, and he says it makes him feel much better.

September 1, 2010. Today was a very long day, since today Brian transferred to Winship Medical Center in Dallas. The head of oncology there, Dr. Albert, was recommended by friends of ours (a couple—he is a Burkitt's survivor) as an outstanding physician. I hope they are right.

All the nurses, techs, and doctors we have become so close to at Hillside stopped by in the morning to say goodbye. It was very sweet—there were tears on many faces, including mine.

Transport arrived. I got to ride in the ambulance with Brian (of course). They said they usually do not allow that, but when do I follow stupid rules? Harold drove his car and Cheryl drove our car packed to the brim with all our stuff.

It was a long trip to Dallas—long and bumpy. I tried so hard to get Brian air ambulance transport, but the insurance didn't think it was necessary. I would like to see someone that makes those decisions at the insurance company be as sick as Brian and not feel they need to go by air.

Finally (after the ambulance driver got lost and had to use the GPS on his phone to find the right road), we arrived at Winship. This place is HUGE. A bit overwhelming, too, especially after I had gotten so comfortable at Hillside.

We met Dr. Albert. He was very nice and took the time to talk to us about this whole journey so far. Cheryl asked me if I brought all my journals with me. I said no—I have all the information in my head. Well, when Dr. A started asking questions about dates and procedures, I blanked! I was thinking to myself, You know this! *Obviously we've been living and breathing this, we've halted our lives for this … I was so frustrated with myself. Dr. A let us know he'll be transferring Brian from the oncology floor to one of the ICUs in order to keep a better eye on him. That transfer will be done later today; I like that things Dr. A asks for get done right away.*

Then Dr. A told Brian he was going to talk to me outside about some medical records. When we were in the hallway and Brian's door was closed, Dr. A looked at me and said, "Brian is very sick …" He doesn't know if he can cure him. Usually with Burkitt's patients, he said, it's a bad sign if they don't go into remission after chemo. If there are no white cells in Brian's bone marrow, there will be nothing he can do. The transplant right now would kill him.

He asked how long we've been married. I told him. He asked about my support system, and I told him about that, too. Then I asked him if he was optimistic. "I'm not optimistic, but I'm never pessimistic," he said. Not the reassurance I was looking for.

I couldn't break down and sob like I wanted to because I had to go back into the room with Brian and I knew he was awake. Cheryl and Harold had gone to get something to eat. When I came back into the room, Brian said "What?" I just said "Oh, nothing," and smiled and rubbed his hand. Man, it was so hard not to bust up crying.

Dr. A approached Brian's parents in the hall to tell them the same thing he told me ... that's when I lost it. I knew I couldn't go back to Brian's room, so I asked a nurse to show me to a bathroom and she actually walked me there herself. Very sweet.

I called the friends who recommended Dr. A. and told them he seemed abrasive and unsupportive, but they said he is just focused on getting patients well and his bedside manner is not great. I think that's a huge understatement.

While all of that was still buzzing in my head, there was still a lot we had to do to get transitioned into life here at Winship:

8:00 p.m. – Chest x-ray.

8:15 p.m. – Breathing treatment.

8:30 p.m. – A nurse wanted to ask me questions about Brian's history. She took the time to sit down and write out the things I told her. I asked her to call the chaplain for me, which she did. She also ordered "magic mouth" solution for Brian's mouth sores and got approval to up his fluids; she noticed he could use some blood tonight, and talked to the doctor about that, too. I like how proactive the nurses here are!

8:45 p.m. – Hospital chaplain came by. She kinda reminded me of my second grade teacher. We went to a small, nice room, where once again I lost it. She told me she sees miracles happen every day, and that no offense to Dr. A, but this is a typical reaction from new patients and caregivers. I felt much more at ease after we talked, and she even said that tomorrow she will be back to give me the "survival tour" – places I'll need to know about in order to get around here while Brian is admitted. I am looking forward to that!

10:05 p.m. – I left to take a shower at my friend Amy's house (she lives 2 minutes away).

12:15 a.m. – When I returned to the hospital, there was a nurse sitting right outside Brian's room. I asked her how things were going and she gave me a full report without any hesitation! While I was gone, Brian got a Neupogen injection to help stimulate the WBC count. They'll be hanging all sorts of anti-fungals, antibiotics, and a unit of blood tonight.

2:48 a.m.—Another breathing treatment. The staff here are so observant; if Brian is asleep, they take care not to turn on every light in the room and are very gentle with him. This comes as such a blessing—it's hard when I don't trust the staff to care for Brian with the consideration I would, and here I feel that will not be an issue. The nurses clue me in to what is going on without seeming angry or frustrated with my questions, and they don't hesitate to spell out names of his medicines when I ask. It is really amazing!

It has been a VERY long day. There's no place to fit my air mattress, so I've pushed two chairs together that I'll be using as a bed. I can't imagine anything less comfortable, except staying awake another minute.

September 3, 2010. Where do I start? It has been a roller coaster to say the least these past few days.

First things first: The chaplain came back the next day and gave me a tour and introduced me to several nice people. I really loved that.

Dr. A is growing on me. I was warned several more times by several different people that I would have to get used to the way things are done here and WOW— have I ever. I think of Dr. A like the Tasmanian devil (and no, I don't mean to comment on his bushy eyebrows!); he comes into the room, always followed by an intern or resident or nurse, checks on Brian rather brusquely, gives his orders, and dashes out again before the dust has time to settle.

Every morning when Brian's lab results come in, the nurses write the numbers on a dry erase board in his room. They keep a week's worth of numbers up. It is pretty neat and very appreciated, as that is something I usually hurry to write down in my journal when the labs are announced.

The nurses are so good here, but I think this has actually made Brian a little perturbed with me. I have not been as active in his care here as I was at Hillside, since things are done right here and I don't feel the need to intervene. I am kinda worn out from the past eight months of doing every little thing ... don't get me wrong, if I see something that needs doing I either chime in or fix it myself, but

I don't feel the same pressure I did at Hillside.

Brian is also experiencing side effects of the radiation. His face is red and his ears are very swollen, almost like wrestler's ears. I think he is having trouble hearing as a result. His skin is also still peeling on his face and head.

We took a big leap of faith coming here but I think we did the right thing. The whole family had a hand in the decision—I didn't want the pressure of that to rest with me alone. We all feel that when you ask God for advice, you don't ignore it. So here we are!

September 4, 2010. WBC at 0.1! That was some great news we got this morning.

There was also not-so-good news: one blood culture came back positive for strep and another came back positive for VRE. Both are treatable bacteria that are pretty commonly contracted when someone has been in the hospital for a long time, but still it is not great considering that Brian needs to get strong. Dr. A says those bacteria are why Brian has been running a low-grade fever since he got here, but I mentioned that Brian always gets a fever after he finishes chemo.

Brian's breathing is getting much better with the breathing treatments, and they also gave him a little suction-thingy here that helps pull the crud out without coughing (which is painful because of the sores in his mouth and throat from radiation).

In other news, our plan for living arrangements down here changed quite a bit. Originally I thought Amy's house would be the perfect place to shower and do laundry (I have my air mattress at the hospital), but now Cheryl and Harold are planning to be down here a lot and can't be checking in and out of hotels all the time. Our insurance company won't help us with housing, so we talked to a social worker who told us about the Many Blessings House. Families of patients who live more than 50 miles away from Winship are eligible for an apartment at Many Blessings.

Anyway, the social worker got it all set up and we got a discount, too! So now we have an apartment to stay in while we're down here, Brian's parents don't have to stay in hotels, and we can have a little feeling of "home" even though we're so far away from Owasso. There's a washer & dryer, galley kitchen, two beds and a living room … such an incredible God-send.

We are just passengers on this train of life. I don't know the destination, but with God as the conductor I know our faith will keep us on the right track. That is all that matters!

September 9, 2010. *Brian was transferred out of the ICU! His new room has a little refrigerator and a private bathroom with a shower. Best of all, it has a pull-out sleeper that turns into a twin bed, so I can have a place to sleep now!*

Judi called today from Dr. S's office. It was great to hear her voice, but she told me that Brian's brother is not a match for the bone marrow transplant. Bummer! Later, Dr. A's bone marrow coordinator came in and said she will do more blood tests on Brian to get the transplant testing started, but Dr. A says he wants to see Brian get stronger physically before he will do much of anything. Eventually they will do a scan and restage him, then "go from there." I voiced my concern about that because time is not good with Burkitt's—it can grow so quickly. But Dr. A said any more chemo could kill Brian in his current state.

The importance of Brian getting up and moving around is more critical than ever! I am trying to motivate him but I think he is tired of my harping. That's where all your cards and encouragement really help, so keep 'em coming!

September 10, 2010. *This morning was very rough. The nurse came in extra-early to draw labs and weigh Brian, and she was asking questions we both thought she should know the answer to if she had read his chart. We tried to get some sleep after she came in, but of course we are doing breathing treatments every 4 hours here (no matter if Brian is sleeping or not). A couple hours later there was another nurse with meds and a print-out of Brian's labs (which I really like!).*

At 11:15 a.m. Dr. A came by. For the life of me, I just cannot read this man. On the one hand, he said Brian is looking better and he'll schedule him for a scan next week to see if the cancer is in remission. On the other hand, he never says anything POSITIVE. It's always "if" or "maybe" with him, and I like to hear "is" and "yes"—positive words that show we have a plan! Haven't heard those from Dr. A yet, and don't feel like I'm being heard at all.

Today I asked Dr. A about getting Brian back on the appetite stimulant he was on at Hillside, Megace. It really helped Brian feel hungry enough to eat the foods he needs to get strong. Dr. A says he doesn't like Megace because of what it does to the liver and just shut me down right away. What do I know? I'm only a wife.

Later, Brian told me that Dr. A scares him to death. Coming from a man with Burkitt's Lymphoma, I think that says a lot.

September 14, 2010. Today Brian had his PET scan bright and early at 7 a.m. If you're not familiar with how a PET scan works, here it is: You get injected with a radioactive sugar, which they let work its way through your body for about 45 minutes. The sugar attaches itself to cancerous cells, so when they put you in the machine the image "lights up" with areas where there's cancer in the body. (Who knew I'd be giving science lessons?!)

Later in the morning Dr. A came in. He said he's been impressed with Brian because he's proving himself to be a lot stronger than he seemed when he first got to Winship. He talked to Brian about how important it is for him to get up and move around as much as possible, and he said he knows it won't be easy or pain-free.

He also told Brian that tomorrow he will do the bone marrow biopsy, then asked if Brian did his exercises today. Brian said he sat in the therapeutic chair for 30 minutes. "Did you call the paper?" Dr. A said. "Call the Tulsa Daily News! Brian Howell sat up in his chair!" We are figuring out that Dr. A is a joker after all, and I am always happy when someone can pal around with Brian and make him smile. Before he left, Dr. A said to Brian: "Your wife and parents told me you were a strong, tough guy before you got sick, so that is what we're going to get you back to."

Finally, positive feedback!! I loved hearing that and have such a good vibe about today. I know in my heart that Brian's cancer is in remission after the last round of chemo at Hillside. Thank you all for your love and support. God is good!

September 15, 2010. After I posted my update last night, Dr. A asked me to come to his office to review the PET scan results … the news was not what we were hoping for. He showed me the scan and said that the major concern right now is the lung, which lit up significantly. They will draw the fluid out *and test it for Lymphoma. There are little spots everywhere, too—especially on Brian's knees.*

Dr. A said he will write for Rituxan, a medicine that is supposed to help reduce the Burkitt's cells, but he also said that Brian is too weak to undergo more chemotherapy. If he gave him any, it would kill Brian. This is a statement the family doesn't understand. We have seen Brian receive chemo in much worse condition than he's in right now; Dr. A is at a disadvantage because he's only meeting Brian now and doesn't know what he's been through.

He said a transplant is not an option since Steve was not a match. They aren't searching the national registry because they have to make sure Brian can have the transplant before making a donor go through everything that needs to be done in order to donate.

He also said that he might send Brian back to Hillside, his "Tulsa home," to be comfortable. That is when I stopped listening. All I could hear was Dr. A throwing in the towel, but I am not ready to do that and neither is Brian! "The outcome for Brian doesn't look good," he said. I wanted to clap my hands over my ears.

I asked if the bone marrow biopsy will take place; Dr. A replied that he won't put Brian through it if he doesn't have to, so we'll wait to get results from the fluid in Brian's lung. If the tests show Lymphoma, "the biopsy will be pointless."

Dr. A finished by telling me that if this were his son, he would do the same thing. He would send him home to be comfortable and at peace.

I wanted to scream: WHAT?! ARE YOU JUST GIVING UP??

Instead I walked to this little room the chaplain showed me and I called Steve. He got Stephanie on the phone, too, and I told them everything Dr. A said. They don't understand why he's giving up—because to them, too, that is what it feels like this doctor is doing. I brought the phone to Brian and Steve tried to motivate him to get up and move around more—prove to Dr. A that he is getting stronger and needs to continue aggressive treatment.

After all that, Brian and I had a heart-to-heart. I bawled my eyes out and told him that I don't want to be alone. I want to have him here with me! I told him he has to start exercising and moving and FIGHTING harder, harder, harder. It was so sad and frustrating to talk to him about this ... Brian told me I am a drill sergeant. I told him it was tough love.

Hayley Howell

Now Brian is asleep. Watching him, I try to think back to when this all began nine months ago. Nine months ... we should be pregnant, getting debt-free, enjoying each other's smiles and talks, reminiscing about our summer vacation to Tennessee. On the weekends he should be mowing the yard and I should be taking him a big ol' cup of water at the halfway point. We should be playing with the doggers and sharing our meals and sleeping in our own bed, in the home we love.

Instead we are miles away from home with what seems like no hope for our future together. It's not just Brian's life that's not looking good ... how can I possibly go on living without him?

Will I have to sell the house soon? Will I have to sell the cars and bikes? Will I have to plan a funeral? Are we leaving Winship defeated? Am I a horrible person to even think about those things right now? So many questions running through my mind and I can't make them stop. Well, I could, but that would require sleeping for a long, long time, and I have vowed to be present for Brian ALWAYS. I never want him to wake up alone or ask where I am — NEVER.

My new hope and prayer: That when we get back to Oklahoma and see Dr. Schaffer, he will have a plan for reevaluating Brian. That we can set things up at home so Brian will be able to stay in his space, his bed, the house he built. That the Rituxan works. That the next scan shows improvement. That Brian will be a survivor. That I will not be left on this earth alone. That God will not take my best friend, my soul mate.

In the Lord's name we pray. Amen.

Chapter Eleven

There is a moment just before the wheels of a plane make contact with the asphalt beneath them when the collective sense of anticipation among the passengers makes it feel as though the whole world is holding its breath. It's hard to tell what people are waiting for—a smooth landing or disaster.

The hush we share deflates as soon as we feel the friction below us and the plane begins a seamless deceleration. Somewhere behind me, there is a smattering of applause. Hank clears his throat.

I watch the world outside slow from a blur to something like fast-forward on a DVD to something like stillness. I realize that the closest I have been to Brian since that haunting September morning was when this plane was at its highest point in the sky. When we were closest to heaven. When I was closest to my heart and so, my home.

September 20, 2010. I never thought I'd know what a DNR is. I never thought I'd have to face these issues, not now at least. I, like all of you, prayed and prayed for the Lord not to take my soul mate from me. I prayed that we could get through this and be able to live a long and happy life together. I prayed that this was all just a bad, bad dream. I prayed for a miracle.

Signing the DNR was ... horrible. Steve saw I was struggling with it and said to me, "Hayley, you don't want these doctors doing what they'd have to do to bring a man back from meeting his Creator." It's true—I don't want to see Brian's ribs get broken or have tubes stuck down his throat. BUT DAMMIT, I WANT MY HUSBAND. So does Jesus, I've been telling myself. I reluctantly signed the form.

Brian hasn't responded to the steroids Dr. A prescribed to treat the dangerously high level of calcium in his body right now. Here are the numbers: Calcium yesterday—11.8. Calcium today—13.6. Normal calcium level—8.5-10.1. Steve explained that hypercalcemia is common in cancer patients because of dehydration and the way certain hormones secreted from the tumors make the patient's bones break down. Then the kidneys get backed up and shut down and after that . . .

Brian is very confused (also due to high calcium level). We're still hoping the steroid kicks in, but he's on a PCA pump—a pain pump—that delivers a strong medicine every hour. He sleeps most of the time. I let myself cry while he's dreaming.

I really hope the steroid works; it would let Brian talk to his friends and family again before meeting our Heavenly Father. I wish I could go with him ... I wish a lot of things. And maybe this is weird to say, but I wish I knew how to act right now. I feel like a dying flower inside, just waiting for all my petals to shrivel up and fall away. Then all the beauty and purpose in my life will disappear, quiet as a whisper. How do dying flowers act? I wish I knew . . .

You all have no idea how hard it is for me to say "pray," but I know deep in my heart that that is what I should do. It is what we should all do. I am praying for Brian to find peace, and for him to be comfortable in the life he has left on earth.

I know that humans are selfish—I am selfish—in that we want our loved ones to remain here with us. But Brian is going to be in a better place soon. He's going to God, and to wholeness, and to a place where cancer doesn't tear people apart. When he is awake, Brian still knows who I am. I hope and pray he always will.

Two days later, the sky dawned clear and the air was so hot I could see ripples rising off the pavement when I looked down to the street from Brian's room. I hadn't slept the night before, and my mom stayed over at the hospital, too. I called Cheryl at the Many Blessings House around 7:00 a.m. and told her she'd better get to Winship. I had an awful, overwhelming feeling. Looking back, I think my heart knew it was about to be broken irrevocably.

If my memories of Brian—our life together, our love—are like a blanket I wrap myself in to stave off a chill that never seems to thaw, then the sounds in his room that morning are like sharp barbs in all that softness. Brian was helpless against the liquid pooling in his throat, his lungs. With his head lolled to one side—almost resting on his shoulder— he choked and gurgled for hours. I am haunted by those sounds, and by the feelings that come with them: helplessness, dread, sadness heavier than the world itself. Greenish slime oozed from his nose and mouth. Every time I wiped it away with a cool, damp cloth, more appeared. I persisted regardless; Brian liked to be neat. I searched the faces of the people around me for an explanation, but no one answered. I don't know if I ever even asked a question.

At some point a nurse arrived and told us a transfer was impossible in Brian's present condition. I could barely hear her over the sounds coming from Brian's throat and my own prayers, muttered quietly aloud but raging at maximum volume in my head. Eventually, I realized a subtle shift had taken place in my mind, from praying that God would save Brian to begging God to take him, painlessly and quietly. I was mortified.

I kept telling Brian that I loved him, that I would be okay, that it was all right for him to go home. A chaplain came and prayed with us; the nurses left us alone. There were six of us there in the room: Cheryl, Harold, Steve, my mom, me, and my soul mate.

Brian's mumbling and gurgling got worse, almost proportionately to the tears the rest of us couldn't hold back. Eventually my mom rested her hand on my shoulder and whispered, "Hayley, can you understand him?"

"No," I told her, "but I'm afraid he has so many things left to say."

"Not so many. Just one. 'Hayley, I love you.'"

I lost myself utterly; I threw myself across Brian's body and screamed my love for him, how badly I wanted to go with him. Some part of me must have thought that God would heed my prayers if only I spoke them loudly enough.

At 9:41 a.m., Brian straightened his head on the pillow and opened his eyes. He looked out—past me, past the ceiling, past the sky—like he saw something, someone. He drew his last breath and I watched his skin turn instantly pale.

I looked at Steve, screamed for him to get help, get a nurse, get anyone! He told me to take my time. I checked Brian's pulse frantically, shook him, cried out, "Babe! No! This wasn't supposed to happen! I want to go with you! Please, I want to go with you!" I am sure now that everyone on the floor could hear me recite what had become the only truth I could understand: *"This wasn't supposed to happen to us. This wasn't supposed to happen to us."*

I looked up to find a nurse standing there, stethoscope in hand. She looked at me with wide, wet eyes, shook her head and said something I didn't hear because the noise in my head was too loud. I thought I was going to be sick and ran to the bathroom, but rushed back to the bed. I hadn't left Brian's side in nine months, I reasoned, and I wasn't going to leave him now. I shut Brian's eyes. His body grew cold.

For the next 30 minutes, I sat there, stunned and heartbroken, hopeful that I would be taken, too. I was overcome by the memory of Brian once asking me if I had ever seen an animal pass away. No, I told him. "It's the strangest thing," he said. "The animal has life in it and then a second later, it doesn't. You can see the life go right out of it. It's there one minute and the next—gone." I marveled at how quickly Brian's skin had turned the palest shade of flesh I'd ever seen. Brian was so smart and always right, so on some level it shouldn't have surprised me that he was right about dying, too. I had witnessed the moment his spirit left his body. I knew it had taken a piece of mine with it.

Dr. A walked in, his manner as brusque and haphazard as usual. "Well," he said, but never finished his sentence. From the corner of my eye I saw him embrace Cheryl. He didn't so much as approach me, and looking back, I'm sure that was one of his more perceptive choices.

Somewhere in the room I heard Cheryl's familiar voice. She was making a phone call, telling the person on the other line that "Brian died."

Those words—"Brian died"—seemed to fill the stark room like a hot air balloon, displacing all the breathable air with poison. My mind was ringing with the phrase, objecting to it, denying it. *Brian didn't die, he passed away to a better life!* I wanted to yell, but I couldn't find the words in my broken heart.

Before I left Winship forever, I had one more request. I asked the nurses to let me be alone with Brian—just Brian, no tubes or beeping monitors or hushed voices. I wanted to see him, to be with him one last time, as if he were just sleeping. After everything we'd been through together, I will never forget the feeling of being in that room with him, together one last time.

Brian lay on the gurney, and when I thought back to that moment when I first saw him waiting for me in that smoky bar, I hardly recognized him. His strong physique had been chipped away to reveal only skin and bones. He was cold. I wanted one last moment together with him, but we weren't together—I was alone. The silence was deafening, and I instantly broke down. This could not be my strong husband with whom I always felt so safe. This was not our life.

After leaving the room, Cheryl asked to go in after me, to see him. I couldn't let someone else make the mistake I had just made; it was a mistake that would haunt me forever. "You don't want to do that. You really don't want to," I told her. She listened, and as quickly as we'd arrived at Winship, we were gone.

I was overcome by a sudden, pervasive need to be free of that room. For nine months, I had lived in a pressure cooker sealed by stress and disease and unspeakable grief, and to hear the repetition of my new, awful reality—"Brian died"—was more than I could bear.

I had to get out.

Chapter Twelve

I *have to get out.*

I have to leave this seat, this plane. Right now, before another single moment passes. Panic rises in my throat. Gagging on it, I realize where I am. I realize it has been 3 months since Brian has passed on, and I still remember it as vividly as if it was happening before me. Every time I replay the scene of Brian's death, I feel like I can lie to myself and change the ending, but I never do. I try to find the best place to change the story, to tweak it so that Brian is still alive, but my mind carries on with the truth, despite my wishes.

People are standing now, slowly being herded like cows toward a door that still hasn't opened. I wish that I could push past them. Seat belts click, yawns trickle through the cabin, and I am trapped—trapped in this plane, trapped in the reality that Brian is dead. I feel hot and nauseous. I am sick. I am sick with grief, sick of being sad, sick of being smothered by the idea that there was more I could have done or something left unsaid. I put one foot in front of the other, following the too-orderly line of passengers as we exit the plane. I glaze over the eyes of strangers, talking into their cell phones, calling loved ones—how can they go on as if life hasn't changed? I feel as though an earthquake has cracked the world in half, and somehow I am the only one who saw it. I am brushing past the navy-clad stewardess and inhaling that wisp of fresh air that exists between the plane and the jetway. Signs, feet, bags, keys, I am moving quickly now, anxious to get anywhere—anywhere that isn't inside my memory.

Finally, finally, I burst out of the airport and onto the street, and find that I am breathing like a woman who was drowning, because that is exactly what I have been doing for a long time.

Eventually my mom led me out to her car. I knew I needed to go, but where? Brian was always telling me that GPS systems are crap, and as we struggled to get out of downtown Dallas that sunny September morning, I couldn't help but think to myself, "Right again, babe."

Finally we were on the road home—though I didn't know if that was even a place anymore. For so long I had told myself that my home would be wherever Brian was, that I would be okay whenever Brian was okay. So where was home now? And how would I ever be anything close to okay?

The whole drive, I stared out the window. I thought about what had just happened. I thought about how many times I told Brian that Winship would be his cure—because I believed it would be. But there I was, leaving without him.

The weather that day was beautiful, so beautiful, on our drive. It was still hot, but so clear and colorful and bright. I thought I could get lost in that perfect sky. All I did was stare out the window for at least 100 miles. Not a word was spoken.

After about an hour, though, my mom said, "You should probably get on Facebook and tell everyone. You know, the people who have been with you the whole way." I knew she was right.

September 22, 2010. My Love is with our Heavenly Father.

As many of you know, Brian went to heaven this morning. I want to thank each and every one of you for all your nice words and prayers over the past nine months.

Brian is and always will be a part of me. I hope and pray he left this earth knowing how much I love him. In his final hours, he kept repeating, "Hayley,

I love you." It was hard to understand, but I could.

All I want is for him to be at peace and I know that he met our Heavenly Father today, which makes me so glad. Brian was a God-fearing man and he taught me so much about God and the Bible.

There will never be another Brian. He was and is my one true soul mate.

Chapter Thirteen

We scheduled the funeral for the following Monday. The days leading up to it were a whirlwind of planning and decision-making and arrangements. No one ever tells you that being a widow means orchestrating a thousand moveable pieces at once, the largest of which is your own grief.

I picked out a sky blue casket—Brian's favorite color—with praying hands embroidered on the inner lid. I insisted that my husband not be buried in a tie. "He wasn't married in a tie, and he won't be buried in one, either," I reasoned. Instead he wore a familiar ensemble: a blue button-down and black slacks with socks and shoes to match. It was what he wore the day we were married. In his pockets I tucked three black tubes of Chapstick. I gave him his Bible—the one he'd read through twice; someone put a letter next to him, too.

Each morning of the viewing, I arrived early to check that Brian looked okay, that the picture of us on a pedestal near the coffin was clean and angled just so. He was wearing too much make-up, which is to say, he was wearing any make-up at all. But Brian's hands were still bruised from his IVs and his skin was so, so white. That was the hardest part—seeing him that way, knowing he'd never come home with me.

My pastor—Pastor Dave—performed the service. "We all experience death in the physical and spiritual sense. Brian knew his physical body wouldn't last forever; whether it was cancer or old age, he knew we all come to an end. But Brian also knew there is Forever to look forward to. So maybe you take a deep breath and think to yourself, 'I can't think of a sadder circumstance for this young bride and this family,' but in the same breath, thank God that we know where Brian is. We know he's safe. 'He will wipe every tear from their eyes,' we read in Revelation, 'There will be no more death or mourning or crying or pain, for the old order of things has passed away.'" Stephanie's father—a preacher in his own right—delivered a eulogy.

Then came the stories.

"I grew up in this church," Steve said. "And we were here one Sunday evening when Brian and I were just kids. There was some kind of children's sermon, and all of us youngsters were supposed to come up front and sit on the steps around the pulpit. Afterwards, we were supposed to go back to our parents. So I got almost to the back pew to rejoin our folks when I looked behind me and saw that Brian wasn't there. In fact, he was still in the front row. Mom said to me, 'Let's leave him there. How much trouble could he get into in the front row in church?' That's when Brian pulled a cap gun out of his pocket, turned around to rest his elbows on the back of the pew, and started shooting at everyone in the immediate vicinity.

"My mother was mortified, naturally, and sent me back up front to fetch my brother. But instead of coming with me—Brian was a bit hard-headed as you might know—we broke out in a fight right there in the center aisle. Mom had to come up front and get us both.

"Another time, my car broke down. I called Brian to come get me, and come he did. He told me we didn't need a tow truck—he'd push me home. I had it in my mind that we'd cruise along with the car in neutral and me steering; at most, I thought, we'd reach 15 miles per hour. Well before I know it, I look at the dash and realize we're going 55 miles an hour in a 30 mile-per-hour zone; *and the car's not even in drive.* I looked in the rear view and saw Brian behind me, wearing the biggest smile I'd ever seen."

There were others, too, who filled the chapel with memories of my husband. A friend of Brian's from Atlanta got up and told a story about a Braves game they went to together. Two cousins stood and recounted Brian's unique, infectious laughter. Cheryl said a few words. Every anecdote seemed to center around a common theme—Brian's passion and gusto for life, his quick wit and quicker laughter.

I remember the sunshine and the cool breeze during the graveside service, and the insistent feeling that I shouldn't sit and wait to be approached by a line of mourners afterward. I wanted to get up and mingle, walk around and thank people for coming, for following us on our journey—even to its dark, heartbreaking end.

There was a dinner back at the church. I couldn't tell you what we served or how long it lasted, though I remember asking the man in charge if I could address everyone assembled before the crowd inevitably dissolved. I'm still not sure where the urge came from, but I felt wholly compelled to say something, offer something to the people with whom I'd shared that day.

"I just want to thank you all for following us on our journey," I said. "A lot of you have asked if there's anything you can do, and there is. You can be good people, good Christians who do for others. And you can take a final lesson from Brian: love each other." I didn't trust my voice to continue. Inside I felt like scattered, dried leaves over the pavement, rolling along in search of soft soil. I just needed a place to rest.

At the end of my first seven days as a widow, I was shocked to look back on the week and realize I had survived. Though my mom or other close family members had stayed with me each night that week, I felt entirely alone, abandoned by my own life.

I was focused on adjusting my thinking to the idea that Brian was fine. In fact, I told myself, he's better than all of us. Though I thought it was selfish, I couldn't help wanting him to hug me and kiss me again. I wanted to smell his skin right out of the shower. I wanted to see his smile. I wanted to argue with him over something totally stupid and have him get on to me for squeezing the toothpaste from the middle. Through all that wanting, I tried to remember not to be selfish—*Brian is whole where he is, healthy and free.*

My main worry during those first weeks was the house. The danger that I would lose the property was very real. If I did, I knew it would be like losing Brian all over again. I suspected that was something I couldn't survive twice.

The house was his home, and I hadn't changed a thing since I'd been back in Oklahoma. I learned quickly that even though the death of a spouse is hard enough, on top of your grief and heartache you have to deal with financial worries. In 20/20 hindsight, I understood the importance of preparing a will. I saw, too, the necessity of talking about "what ifs" before tragic possibilities become reality. I tried so hard to keep positive around Brian that we never really talked in-depth about what would happen if he passed. The very idea of that was so outrageous to me that I refused to entertain the possibility I'd be going back home alone.

I prayed that Brian would be pleased with all the decisions I made. I hoped he liked his casket and the burial site I chose for him. I wondered if he'd be okay with me sleeping on his side of the bed. I wondered if he'd want me to keep on living in the house without him.

My worries for the past nine months had been enormous. That hadn't changed. Only the scale of enormity changed; the sky is enormous, but mountains are, too.

Everyone kept telling me to take it one day at a time. Well, I felt rushed. I felt rushed to get back to work because I wanted to keep the house and to do that, I had to prove my income. I felt rushed to put down my sadness and live, as I know Brian would have wanted me to do, but I couldn't find the strength to do that just yet.

Most nights, I would sit alone at home. The doggers would keep me company as usual. One morning, after I went to church, I came home and cleaned the house a little and did some paperwork. I dozed off on the couch, and just when I was in that hazy place between dreaming and waking up, I had the strongest certainty that Brian would be home any minute and we would decide what to have for dinner.

"Alone" is not about not having people around you. "Alone" is deeper than a physical presence or lack of one; it's the absence of a soul presence that I felt. It's hard to explain.

Even the dogs seemed lonely.

October 6, 2010. Today was my first day back at work after not "working" for the past nine months. I am truly grateful to my employers for offering me back my position, but even returning to something familiar was so hard.

I bought a voice recorder the other day because when I drive, I think, and want to record some of my thoughts for use in the book. I know the book is something Brian believed in, so I must pursue it relentlessly. I know that. The more I remember details from the past nine months, the more I can hear Brian's voice echoing the phrase he used throughout our journey: "Hayley, did you get that?" Sometimes, while I was scribbling away in my journals at his bedside, Brian would take a long look at whatever nurse was doing whatever test and say: "She's writing a book about all this, you know. You'll probably be in it." Brian wanted the book. He wanted our story told. I'm the only one left to tell it.

I hate music at the moment—it all makes me cry. So in the car I just talk and talk—to God, to Brian, to myself. I feel officially crazy, but I think in some small way it helps.

Around 9:40 a.m. this morning I did all I could to keep my mind from thinking about what happened two weeks ago today. To make matters worse, the day seemed to drag on and on. Fortunately, though, the usual Wednesday meeting was canceled and I got to go home fairly early. Four hours back on my first day didn't seem so terrible ... until I left the office. Usually that's when I'd call Brian to let him know I was coming home. Today I just cried the whole way back to the house. How am I ever going to get back to normalcy? What does that even mean anymore?

October 9, 2010. What does "therapeutic" mean to you? To me it's riding a motorcycle. I didn't think getting out on the bike with the wind in my hair would feel as good as it did. I was shocked by how much I missed that feeling of freedom and possibility. But there it was, waiting for me just as it always has been.

I know Brian was with me as I cruised around town yesterday. "Go park it!" I could hear him saying. I grinned to myself at points in the ride when I knew Brian would have been laughing at me—when we would have been laughing together.

Brian taught me how to ride. He was a trainer at his job and was such an amazing teacher in all things. One of the things I'll miss most is Brian teaching me something new every day. I didn't think I'd remember all his words of wisdom out on the bike, but just like freedom, Brian's voice was there for me, too. I missed trading the special hand signals we used while riding; I made the motions anyway, since I knew Brian was watching.

The world is still spinning, and other humans here keep living. Everyone goes on with their lives and somehow, I know I must do this, too. But I don't want to move on. I want to remember and remember and remember, even though thinking like that will get me nowhere and I know it.

October 24, 2010. *Brian's 36th birthday. Tonight at 5:00 p.m., Brian's family and I went to his grave. His nephews drew some pictures and wrote a note; I wrote a note, as did Cheryl. Steve and Stephanie brought a card. We tied everything to balloons—blue ones, of course—and up, up, away they went. Stephanie's father led us in prayer, and helped us all realize that Brian is still very much alive and WELL. All we have to do here on earth is what we must to join Brian in eternity … and life is just a vapor compared to eternity.*

I believe with all my heart that through Christ, I will see my husband again.

By the end of October, I was convinced that I was failing at grief. I could not seem to get a handle on it; Brian was all I thought about, all I wanted to think about. I wanted to see him so badly, I was sure my hurt was more than anyone is meant to bear.

I had begun to forget everything. I had to write myself notes in order to remember to do the simplest things. If you've ever known someone who underwent chemotherapy, you might have heard them talk about "cancer brain"—very forgetful. Well I came to think I had "widow brain." My stress level and emotions and anxiety were all so overwhelming that I couldn't keep the slightest thought in my head for long. Except for the thought of how much I missed my husband. That thought I could not forget.

I started seeing a grief counselor. She helped me realize that grief is a roller coaster; one week I would be in a valley, which is "perfectly normal." That didn't necessarily make me feel better—because what's normal about your soul mate being ripped from your life at the age of 35, anyway?—but it was nice to hear that other people in my position had experienced something similar.

The counselor gave me a printout titled "The Six Needs of Mourning":

1. Accept the reality of the death.
2. Let yourself feel the pain of your loss.
3. Remember the person who died.
4. Develop a new self-identity.
5. Search for meaning.
6. Let others help you—now and always.

I contemplated the six points carefully, methodically. What did I know for sure about my needs, my mourning? For one, it was hard for me to understand that Brian would never walk through the doors of our home again. Second, I was afraid to let myself feel the pain of losing him, because I didn't think I'd even fully understood that he was gone. I was terrified to feel an emptiness more complete than what I had already felt, so how could I surrender myself to exploring the deepest ends of my pain? The third need was easy—I remembered Brian all day long.

Finding "me" again seemed an impossible task. If you had asked me a year prior, "Hayley, who are you?" I would have said, "I'm Brian's wife." And what did I say for months and months when people asked me how I was doing? "I'll be fine when my husband is fine." The trouble is, I knew that Brian was fine where he was—so fine, and whole and happy in Heaven. But my repeated promise made a liar out of me. I was not fine. I would say that I was anything but fine.

In my heart, Brian was as alive as he ever was. No matter how loudly my brain screamed "Brian is gone! You are alone!" my heart refused to hear it. My heart still believed that I was a wife, not a widow. My heart still believed it had a home.

"Search for meaning." Did that mean asking God why this happened? I vowed not to do that, as it seemed completely impractical. God's plan is for Him to know, not for me to question. But I supposed there were other ways to look for meaning in all that passed, in the sense that everything to stem from it would be connected to Brian and his illness. Still, a part of me didn't want to search for meaning—or rather, a part of me didn't want to need to search for it. I felt like if I could accept things as they are, somehow things would get better.

The final item, "Let others help you." Believe it or not, for a stubborn gal like me, this was the most difficult "need" to satisfy. In a Facebook note, I mentioned that riding the motorcycle was incredibly therapeutic for me. One morning, I planted a mum that someone had given me at Brian's funeral. I broke off one piece and planted it in the back yard, then took the majority of it and planted it in the front of the house. It was a beautiful experience, putting something in the earth. I hoped it would survive.

Chapter Fourteen

November 22, 2010. *Last week I had an interview with a great company. The interview went extremely well, but I didn't want to get my hopes up. Brian always said not to expect too much, so that when something great happens it is truly a wonderful blessing. So that's exactly what I did.*

The very next day I was offered the position! How great is that? This is absolutely an answered prayer — a full-time, salaried position that will help me hang on to the house and support myself.

Of course any happy moment is instantly bittersweet. I want to call Brian and share my news; I want his feedback and advice. I want him to come shopping with me to pick out nice clothes. He'd be especially proud of me for needing those, because I'm so small now, none of my old clothes fit.

The holidays are coming. Thinking about driving to family events alone is depressing.

If it were up to me, I'd skip to the year when I turn 85. That sounds about right, doesn't it? That way I'd be able to skip all the holidays, all the "firsts" I'll have to face ... really, I just want to skip my whole life. But I know I have a choice to make.

My choice is I can either go crawl up in bed and never get out or I can stay positive and put on a smile and be cheery going to my new job and live each day like it's my last. I have a choice to spread the word about Brian's journey. I have a choice to fight to keep our home. Choices, choices, choices ... so many that I get sent right back to missing Brian, wishing he were here to help me decide.

Still, as I go through this week I am determined to start my "new normal." I am going to make positive, meaningful, Christ-like choices. Tomorrow is a new day; I can be happy or sad. I can beat myself up about the mistakes I make or I can forgive myself. I can choose to be defeated or stand tall and believe in myself. I know I will have my moments, but I can honor Brian by being the best person I can possibly be while I have the chance, and hopefully soon I'll be with my love once again.

November 28, 2010. Thanksgiving has just come and gone, and as you might imagine, it was extremely difficult. Instead of laughing and carrying on great conversations with my soul mate en route to a big turkey dinner, I cried most of the way. Instead of talking about how sick and stuffed we were on the way home, I cried again. I always thought only old people carried tissues in their cars. Now I know that old people and widows do.

I feel disconnected with most of the people in my family, like I am the pink elephant in every room. Being surrounded by so many loved ones and feeling so isolated makes the loneliness more prominent.

Today I heard that a young guy I went to high school with, who was a couple of years younger than me, died in a horrible car accident last night. I believe he was married and probably had children. When I hear things like that, I ask God, "Why not me? Why someone with a family and a purpose and motivation to wake up every day? Why couldn't I take that young man's spot and let him live a full life with his family?" In a way it upsets me. And in another way it makes me wonder what I am destined to achieve here on earth.

There has to be a reason, right? Well, when I'm not having a good day and miss Brian so much it physically hurts, I think about those things. I feel like I am ready to meet my Lord and Savior. I have written out my last wishes. I have already had the truest love imaginable in this life, and completed my most noble task: taking care of Brian. What else is left?

The truth is, I would never take my own life, because if I did, I'd never be able to see Brian again. I have to become as Christ-like as I can in order to spend eternity with my husband. I just can't wait for that day to hurry up and get here.

I am learning that there is no timeline for grief. One day I feel like I move forward, the next day I fall ten steps back. I am also learning that the only

solution to this hopelessly circular state is to give it to God. I give Him my
worries, my praise, my problems, and my heart.

At my new job, I would go out to my car every day at lunch to "get well." That was what I called it, anyway. There was a church service on the radio at that time that really helped me. I felt like the preacher was talking directly to me, giving me strength in my faith.

One of the ladies at the office approached my desk one day.

"Hey, Hayley. You going anywhere for lunch?" she asked. "Me and some of the other girls just wanted to extend you an invitation to sit with us in the kitchen. We're all a kind of family here and … well, we just thought you should know you're welcome."

It was a kindness I needed, but I had to refuse. "For right now I think it's best for me to get a little fresh air in the middle of the day."

She said she understood, and I think she really did.

My nights were especially hard.

The devil put awful thoughts into my head, like did I do everything the right way when Brian was sick? Did I tell him everything I wanted to tell him? Could I have done something differently to make life easier for Brian? Did he know what was happening? Should we have talked more about death? Was transferring him to Winship the right decision?

Visions of Brian when he first got sick flooded my mind. I could see him when he first went to the hospital. I saw him when he was getting chemo. I saw his face when I would take his temperature. I saw his eyes when he told me he loved me. I saw him having seizures. I saw him as we loaded up to go to Dallas. I replayed September 22, 2010, over and over and over in my head. I heard the sounds, saw the room, saw his face. I relived it, all of it, every day.

But then, mercifully, I would think about the times before Brian got sick. I thought about our normal routine: him getting ready for work in the morning, him perching on the edge of the bed to put his socks on (even though it woke me up every time!), him getting his boots from the garage and putting them on in the kitchen, him coming in to kiss me before heading off to work.

I always got up to kiss Brian when he got home from work. I remember his smell then, too. I would have a clean towel waiting for him in the bathroom, since he always went straight there to shower after coming home. I remember his smell when he'd get out of the shower, so different from the first smell, but still Brian.

November 30, 2010. Today I looked up from my desk at work. I saw Brian! Yes, this sounds crazy, but it's true. There was a guy about Brian's size with the same hair (or lack thereof)—just like Brian. I took a double take, but it wasn't Brian. Of course it wasn't. My heart skipped a beat anyway. My heart doesn't understand what happened to us.

In two weeks I'm going out to visit my cousin and his wife in Arizona. It will be a test to see if I can be okay away from home. Home is where I'm free to miss Brian, where I can take comfort wearing one of his shirts to sleep and cry whenever I feel like it. I need a test. This safe bubble cannot last forever, and even though it hurts, I must stretch and grow. With Brian by my side I knew I could do anything. Without him, I suddenly question everything—"Can I go to the store? What if I don't get everything? Can I get gas in the truck? What if I choose the wrong kind of gas?" He had been my crutch and I would proudly be lame forever if it meant I could still have him. But it's time to face the music. I need a test.

I have always loved the idea of traveling all over the world. I still think I'd like to do some mission trips and go see a different country ... but for now we'll see how it feels to travel to Arizona. We'll see what God has in store for me there—because I'm on the path He chooses, wherever it takes me.

It's nighttime. Night in the desert is different than night in Oklahoma. It's as though you have been eating peaches your whole life, but one day you eat a fresh, perfect peach—and then you know what a peach is supposed to taste like. That is how night feels in Arizona, it's as though you're finally seeing what God intended. Tonight each star looks like its own little shining world, and I like to think that on one of them, or maybe all of them, Brian and I have a family. He is grilling steaks in the backyard and I am seasoning up the coleslaw in the kitchen. Our daughter runs by with a cherry popsicle, laughter fills the air. I wish more than anything I could live in that world.

Back on Earth, I've pulled off the highway and am lying on the hood of my rented red convertible. I have always wanted to be the girl with the red convertible, and for this trip—this test—I wanted to try it on. I am trying on a life that isn't mine. I take my wedding ring off and move it to my right hand ring finger. Like the car, it doesn't feel right, it feels like I'm just trying it on. My mind nags "Put it back, put it back where it belongs!" but I leave it, knowing I must struggle to accept its new position.

Alone in the desert, on the hood of that car, I know something; being in that plane and cruising at 30,000 feet, I was closer to Brian than I have been in months. Why had I wished it over so soon? I should have relished being up there, being closer to him. And now I am back on the ground again, looking at the stars—twinkling worlds that could've been.

"Don't think of what could've been, Hayley, think of what you can still be," I hear Brian whisper softly to the desert night. I know he is right. Though I must continue on without him, I will never forget how he impacted me. He was my soul mate, my one true love, and I tried never to take a moment with him for granted. Now I have the chance to help people—help people struggling with this disease, help people see how lucky they are to have each other, help people learn to love each other.

Heaven is longer than a plane ride away and you won't be able to travel there, or send letters there to let your love be known. Let it be known out loud every day. Love is the glue that holds the world together, the soap that cleanses away the hatred and yes, even the medicine that cures disease. Even after our journey has ended, what is left of us is love.

Epilogue

April 17, 2011. *Friday was another one of my "firsts." For those of you who don't know, Brian and I were married on April 15, 2008. Friday would have been our third wedding anniversary.*

I knew it was going to be a hard day for me, as are all the days that commemorate special moments that just Brian and I shared. No one else in the family married Brian or had that special time with him—it was just me. It's a day I will have to face again and again on my own. But I knew it would be that way.

Three years ago Friday I became the happiest woman on the face of the planet. It's hard to remember that woman after all that's happened. In a lot of ways, I feel like she never existed. The sadness I felt Friday was bigger than me, bigger than our anniversary. In fact, it was probably the saddest day I've had since the funeral; I felt like the loneliest woman in the universe.

Like I've always said, Brian is where we all want to be. How selfish would it be for me to wish him back here, where he could never be whole? But Friday I was feeling mighty selfish, let me tell you! Sometimes I want to hold him so badly my arms ache. Friday I wanted to kiss Brian and have us get dressed up and hear him say, Happy Anniversary, Babe!

Instead I left work around 12:30 p.m. I was barely able to stay at my desk for 30 minutes at a time in the morning, before having to excuse myself to go bawl my eyes out in the bathroom. I promised myself I wouldn't turn on my phone or participate in any social media on Friday, either—so I was truly alone with my loneliness. It was not a good feeling.

When I left work, I went to Brian's grave. The truth is, I don't actually think of Brian as being there necessarily. Yes, his body is there. But Brian's not. He could never be contained that way—his personality was always bigger than life, and I can only imagine that his soul is even greater and more boundless now that it is free. Still, the headstone is set, engraved with a picture that Cheryl and

I chose. It's good to see Brian's beautiful face, and even though I talk to him all the time anyway, it feels good to look at him when I have important things to say. I took Brian's blue fleece blanket with me—the one my mom made him—in case it was nice enough to sit and stay awhile, but the day was cold and rainy.

I decided some time ago that I would commemorate our anniversary by doing something Brian and I loved to do together: drive. So that's exactly what I did. I hopped in the car and put more than 300 miles on it without worrying about where I'd end up or if I'd get lost. Of course, Brian was always the one who would drive us everywhere ... but I know he is in the car with me whenever I'm behind the wheel.

I drove and drove and went through some interesting towns. You'll never guess what I happened upon, either: a big white trailer with the words HOWELL'S PUMP SHOP painted on it in big, shadowed letters. It would be hard to say if the sign were "a sign" of anything particularly profound, but I kinda felt like God and Brian were doing what they could to bring a smile to my face today. Like anything either of them set themselves to, it worked.

I got home around 8 p.m. and rented a movie I thought Brian would have liked. The doggers climbed into my lap and we had a good time.

Dates—especially ones that were special to me and Brian as a couple—will always be hard for me, I think. Today I couldn't help but think about how all I wanted growing up was to be a great wife and mother. I hope I was a good wife. As far as motherhood goes, the doggers seem to think I'm doing okay, and that's just fine with me.

Acknowledgements

I would like to thank first and foremost my Heavenly Father for blessing me with my soul mate, Brian E. Howell. And for providing such grace and strength to me to continue on.

I would also like the thank my mom, Barbara Adams, and Mike Adams. My in-laws, Cheryl and Harold Finkenbinder, Steve, Stephanie, Preston Jacob and Hope Howell, Fran and Dan Thompson. Pastor Dave, Lynn Sorenson, The Kroh Family, The Wolkins Family, Jake Christensen, Ivan and Barbara Quandel, Jill Quandel-Stanfill, Amber Quandel, Lisa Wolkins, Justin Ransbottom and Family, James and Lynette Blevins and Family, The Dreckman Family, Tory Bartlett and Family, Tommy Yardy and Family, Nurse Jodi, Dr. Alan Langerak, UPT/OTL, Dan and Sharon Shiedel, Donna and Vic Bond, Jeff Runyan, Cheryl Winship and Family, Stuart and Candace Smartt, Sandy Dyke, Ed and Cindy Chapko, the oncology nurses at Baylor, Nurses in ICU 6th floor in Tulsa, everyone who donated to Brian's fund, and thank you to everyone that has supported Brian and I on this journey. All the love and prayers have brought me through such a very difficult, life changing experience. I would also like to thank Burkitt's Lymphoma Society for providing such a great resource to patients and their families.

I would also like to thank my husband, my soul mate, my best friend, Brian. I never thought I would be finishing this book without you, but you are whole and happy where you are and I cannot wait to meet you in Heaven. Thank you for teaching me everything you did! I love you Brian Howell!!

"To the world you may be one person, but to one person you may be the world."

For more information and resources about Burkitt's please visit
www.burkittslymphoma.org

For resources for young widows please visit
www.widowspique.org

About the Author

Hayley Howell lives in Owasso, Oklahoma with her "doggers." She is supported by her family and by her unwavering faith in the fact God has a plan. As a motivational speaker, she speaks to groups regarding grief, cancer, and the healing power of God.

To contact her about a speaking engagement, call (918) 639-4226.

Made in the USA
Charleston, SC
16 October 2015